WANDERING THE HILLS IN A KILT

Stewart Logan

Sue & Dave,

Keep enjoying the hills and wishing you all the best.

Stewart

First published in 2023

ISBN 9781399946049

Design and typeset by Jeremy Fenton

Printed and bound in Great Britain by BookPrintingUK

This book is dedicated to the memory of Bill Hayley with whom I had so many great days in the hills over nearly 40 years during which time we climbed all of Munro's Mountains and subsidiary Tops together.

CONTENTS

Foreword 3

Introduction 5

Chapter 1 Scotland

- 1.1 English Border to Central Scotland 7
- 1.2 Kintyre & Cowal to Tyndrum & Glen Lyon 11
- 1.3 Tyndrum to Glen Coe 20
- 1.4 Fort William to Kingussie 29
- 1.5 Around the Cairngorms 39
- 1.6 Morvern to Glen Carron 51
- 1.7 Glen Carron to the North Coast 66
- 1.8 The Islands 79

Chapter 2 Furth of Scotland

- 2.1 England 89
- 2.2 Wales 94
- 2.3 Ireland 97

Chapter 3 Europe

- 3.1 Around the Alps 100
- 3.2 Norway 110

Chapter 4 Africa

- 4.1 Morocco 112
- 4.2 Tanzania 119

Chapter 5 Asia

- 5.1 Nepal 126
- 5.2 Singapore 134

Chapter 6 Oceania

- 6.1 New Zealand 135
- 6.2 Australia 140

Chapter 7 North America

- 7.1 South-west United States 144
- 7.2 The John Muir Trail 153

Chapter 8 Hill Access and Other Things 161

Chapter 9 Ten Rounds of Munros & Beyond 171

Chapter 10 A.E. Robertson Centenary 176

Chapter 11 Thoughts on Munro's Tables 179

Epilogue 181

Appendix 1 My Hill Lists Completions 183

Appendix 2 Hills Out of Munro's Tables 184

Appendix 3 Hill & Weather Statistics 187

Acknowledgements 188

Foreword

Hamish M. Brown

Stewart Logan was/is an indefatigable hillgoer and, like all such, has a fund of stories about the good days and more memorable epic days that are the hillman's lot. In this collection of anecdotes he happily shares with us some of these incidents and encounters and we are happy to read about them – and hear the laugh that was wont to accompany many in the telling. If Stewart makes it all sound fun, so it was, so it is. This is why we head to the hills. Forget all highfaluting analysing and reasoning; we enjoy, and suffer, for the rare pleasure of simple joy. We know how to celebrate afterwards as many of Stewart's stories indicate.

Stewart is most notoriously known for compleating, at that time, a unique tenth round of the Munros to welcome in the millennium, and in so doing, tailing the twentieth century as AER (Archibald Eneas Robertson, the first Munroist) had topped it in 1901. We are not told whether- as AER – he kissed the cairn and his long-suffering wife on this completion. Like many who have had a lifetime in hills (to a Scot that includes mountains) he records a few mishaps, even tragedies, but that he still admits to being hale(ish) and hearty in his eighties is an excellent recommendation for going on the hills (not necessarily to complete list after list so avidly). Hillgoing is in fact relatively safe. The most dangerous moments of our lives are those in the car. His being older now gives the rest of humanity the new experience of not trying to keep up with Stewart on the hill. At the end of the book there's a sort of statistical account of his doings and some thoughts on Munros and Munroing.

The stories also take Stewart furth and further afield: Alps, Africa (north and south of the Sahara), Nepal, the Antipodes, USA, where the kilt gained many advantages over Sassenach companions. The longest account is of the intricacies of the John Muir Trail in the Sierra Nevada. Most stories are about the quirky species, people and reactions to Stewart's patriotic wearing of the kilt.

The kilt plays a large part in the anecdotes both at home and abroad, something I recognise from replication. I grew up a kilty ("Kilty, kilty, cauld bum"); at school dancing (co-ed) on Fridays, church parade on Sundays and games-away travelling, all so garbed quite apart from roaming the 'home' Ochils. I've Stewart's permission to end with one kilt anecdote of my own.

At Oban youth hostel one holiday in my teens, I was enrolled by a hard-pressed tourist officer because I was Scottish and wearing my kilt. He needed couriers for bus tours laid on for sailors off visiting US warships. "Never mind how much you know. You can always make up stories about any place." The circular tour ran Oban – Crianlarich – Arrochar – Inveraray – Oban, which I knew quite well, thank you. In Glen Kinglas a herd of Highland cows was spotted grazing the slopes and a photo stop demanded. ("Say, boy, do all your cows wear winter-woolies?"). Highlanders certainly look impressive but I assured the sailors they were docile enough so there was a rush uphill. Highlanders are pretty safe but they are very nosey so began to advance downhill to meet the Yanks, who then began to retreat somewhat. Before long there was a rout: the sailors running for the bus and the curious cows trundling after. I received very few tips that evening.

We all have our stories. This collection is perfect for dipping into, for bedtime reading, as a 'bus' book, to be savoured malt by malt. Slàinte.

Introduction

I was born and brought up in Kirriemuir which is two miles from Sir Hugh Munro's family estate at Lindertis. In these far off days I was unaware of Munros although my interest in the hills had started when I used to go grouse-beating in the Angus glens. It has always been a regret that I used to see Sir Hugh's son Torquil shopping in Kirriemuir and wonder what stories about his father I could have learnt from him. Sixty years later it was with great pride and pleasure that I enjoyed a two-year spell as President of The Munro Society.

I have been wandering the hills for over seventy years now and over that time have had many varied experiences. Many of my friends and colleagues, who have had to put up with my tales in the pub after a long day out, have encouraged me to put pen to paper. I hope that this book is entertaining and informative. The stories take you on a journey from the south of Scotland to the north and the islands before moving further afield, after which I discuss the Munros in more detail. Individual hills are mentioned in the tales because I think that, like me, many people will enjoy the stories more when they can associate with an area. I should mention in passing that the spelling of many mountains and features has changed over the years. I have mainly used the spelling current at the time of each tale. My first love is the Scottish hills but, especially since I have retired, I have seen more of the world, and some of the stories reflect this.

I wear the kilt a lot when travelling abroad, except where it is against the local culture, and in the local hills, except where it would be a winter health hazard! Kilt, crampons and axe make a fine sight in the hills when it is not too cold.

I do not make the usual disclaimer of the resemblance to living persons being purely coincidental. In fact, without the various friends, acquaintances and strangers who made the stories possible, there would be few to tell. I would especially like to thank the members of my club, the Clyde Valley Mountaineering Club, who have been a rich source of tales. In reading through my logs in preparing this book, I was struck by the number of occasions that adverse comments on gales, lashing rain, extreme cold, deep snow, whiteouts, vicious spin-drift, mist, flies, midges etc. appeared. However, these events are offset by glorious scorching days with no wind or by wonderful cloud inversions. There may be fewer of the really good days but they make it all the more worthwhile.

I have been collecting these stories for many years. For a few years in my late seventies I was the archivist for The Munro Society. I realised that many present members were reluctant to donate log-books or other material whilst they were still with us but I found it to be rather insensitive to approach families after a death. Now that I am well into my eighties and only getting into the hills occasionally, I feel that now is the time to document some of my experiences over the years.

Chapter 1 Scotland

1.1 English Border to Central Scotland

Many people, myself included, have rather too often forsaken the Southern Uplands of Scotland for the bigger hills further north. The area is not so rugged yet has some very deep and steep-sided valleys which should be treated with respect, especially in winter. The ground tends to be softer and I favour visiting the area when the ground is firm after a hard frost. The hills being lower, there is a better chance of good visibility on high.

Border Crossing

I had summited on the Cheviot with great difficulty. It now has a raised walkway to the trig-point but I had to wade through a morass of eroded and very wet and deep peat. The trig point was quite a sight sitting, as it was, on a column of concrete emerging from the gooey mess. It was very misty but I decided to walk west along the national boundary to Windy Gyle to extend the day.

The boundary fence was an excellent route marker in the conditions so I followed it in a bit of a dream and was a bit surprised when I suddenly heard voices nearby in the mist. I moved towards the sound and found three gentlemen standing on the English side of the fence in casual non hill-walking clothes. When I spoke to them their English was quite poor but they said that they had come from an outdoor centre on the English side of the border and were out for a walk.

They asked me if I was in Scotland and whether they were still in England. When I replied in the affirmative, they silently climbed over the fence and shook my hand. They then re-climbed the fence back into England. As they disappeared back into the mist, they thanked me and said that they were very happy to have visited Scotland. As I went on my way, I reflected that some tourists do not put much into the local economy.

The Lumbering Giant

I was out walking on some of the lesser hills in the Southern Uplands with Hugh and Paul. Now, Paul has the reputation of being slightly ungainly and this trip did no harm to that reputation.

We were approaching the summit cairn on one of the hills and just short of it had to climb a drystane dyke (wall). Hugh and I carefully crossed it and were followed by Paul. He launched himself off the top and a three-foot section of the wall collapsed behind him. We proceeded to do some rebuilding. Coming off the hill down a firebreak, there was some wet-looking ground ahead with a topping of bright green sphagnum moss and Hugh and I instinctively moved slightly aside. Paul kept straight on and went up to his thighs in water and peat. His struggles seemed to be settling him deeper in so, once we had stopped laughing, we grabbed a shoulder each and heaved him out. He was made to change before being allowed into the car.

Rising Fear

I was climbing some of the hills near Dumfries and, as the day progressed, the wind had got stronger and stronger. I approached my last hill of the day, Mochrum Fell. There were no gates at the end of the public road and I was able to take the car onto the forestry track which was shown as circling the hill. I drove along for a bit seeing nothing but impenetrable woods above me. I came to a section which had been cleared below the road and saw some forestry workers planting new trees. I walked down to them and asked if there was a clear way to the top. “There was not,” they said, but they directed me to an area which had been felled partway to the top. I would then have to search for a firebreak.

I found the recommended starting point and fought my way over the tree cuttings to the edge of the upper wood. There was a half-hearted firebreak and I got myself up to a well-hidden trig point at the top. The wind had, by this stage, reached gale-force and, as I descended, I felt movement under my feet. I looked around. The trees were swaying so much that they were trying to tear their roots out of the ground which was moving up and down by over a foot. I have never run out of a wood so fast.

Right or Wrong Hill Name

I was planning to do a round of some of the Lowther hills. It was in the days before GPS so I stopped at a cottage to check that I had got to my planned starting-point. I knocked at the door and a gentleman answered.

“Is that Louise Wood Law up behind your cottage?” I asked.

He laughed. “I think you mean Lousy Wood Law and, yes it is.”

The weather was pretty miserable and, certainly on that day, the hill lived up to its name.

Baa, Humbug

On one occasion I was climbing two hills not far from Abington. I reached the summit of the first on a glorious day when the second hill was clearly seen about two miles west and I started down a ridge to the bealach or col. There were some sheep and lambs off the ridge-line and I took my time and kept well clear of them and, so far as I could see, did not disturb them. As I reached the bealach and started up the slopes of the second hill, I saw a quad bike racing over the hillside apparently aiming to intercept me – which it did.

"What do you think you are doing racing down that hillside opposite and scattering all the sheep? The lambs could run off and die," said the shepherd. I politely answered that I had walked down slowly and was not aware of disturbing the animals but was told that I could not see what I had done. This was in very clear weather where I could see that no animals appeared to have moved.

After more huffing and puffing he then asked what on earth I was doing out on the hills on such a terrible day. This left me somewhat flabbergasted as I pointed out that there was not a cloud in the sky. "Well," he said, "it was bucketing at 6 o'clock this morning."

A Tangled Tale

A party of us had met at Girvan to take a boat trip out to climb Ailsa Craig. However, it was far too stormy for the boat to put to sea so we decided to nip up and down Troweir Hill behind the town.

The hill is double-topped and the first one was reached with no bother. However, the second one was guarded by a barbed wire fence just short of the cairn. I went to cross this obstacle but, in the strong wind, my kilt got totally caught up on the barbs and I was rather stuck with my toes on the ground on either side. The men thought that this was a great laugh and it was much to my embarrassment, and a little pleasure, that it was the ladies who came to my rescue with much fumbling around my knees.

In the hills I am constantly asked the eternal question about what I wear under the kilt. I maintain the secret but promise to do handstands at midnight. Of course, I make myself scarce before then; except once when Club members rushed me and held me upside down in front of the lady members present.

Not Quite the Roof of the World

Peter and I decided to have a winter walk in the Campsie Fells north of

Glasgow. The hill-road over to Fintry was blocked after a heavy snowfall so we went up the south slopes from Lennoxtown and over to Meikle Bin. I had an unfortunate incident at the summit because a strong gust of wind blew a toggle on my anorak hood right into my eye and knocked out a contact lens. In the strong wind and with the ground covered in snow, there was no point in searching for it.

We decided to go west to hit the Fintry hill-road and descend from there back to our car. We approached the dip where the road crossed the ridge. It was hard work in the very deep snow and we encountered funny echoing noises under our feet with a drop in front of us. We negotiated our way around this obstacle and found that we had been standing on the roof of a van totally covered by the drifts. We agreed that the sign in Lennoxtown stating that the road was closed was very accurate!

In the last few years, I have been climbing lists of hills such as Marilyns and Humps of which many, like those in the Campsies, are at quite a low altitude. This has introduced a new element in hill-walking. Many of the lower hills are bounded by golf-courses with the associated risk of flying golf-balls.

1.2 Kintyre & Cowal to Tyndrum & Glen Lyon

For me, the great advantage of this area is that it can all be reached from my home base in little over an hour allowing me to assess the weather and be on the hills soon after breakfast. Many of the hills tend to be very quiet but, with nature all around me, I have never had any problems with solitude in the hills

Who Goes There?

I was going to our static caravan near Dunoon to do some work. I decided to go the long way via the Rest and Be Thankful to take in some lower hills near Loch Long. The first hill was on the road from the submarine base at Faslane to the naval base at Coulport. I had difficulty parking near the hill as the road was lined with crash-barriers but I eventually found a gap where I could park the car. I climbed the very easy hill getting great views over to Faslane from the top. When I got back down to my car, two naval security police were waiting in their Land Rover beside it. They wanted to know what I was doing there and I was able to show them the entry for the hill in my copy of More Relative Hills of Britain.

Things could then have got nasty as they asked me to confirm my name. They pointed out that they had contacted the DVLA at Swansea and this was not my car. I then explained that I had just exchanged my car in Hamilton a few days before. Luckily they had the address of the previous owner who also lived in Hamilton so they sent me on my way with a request not to park on that road again.

I had a similar experience near Scarborough. I drove a short distance past a government establishment to go up a very simple hill. The rain suddenly started lashing so I waited in the car for it to blow over. A Land Rover appeared and the driver asked me what I was doing. He had seen me through binoculars. He too was happy with my explanation and, by now the rain had stopped, so I went up the hill and was quickly away to my next objective.

A Flying Visit

I had come over Ben Vane and Beinn Ime and was now topping Beinn Narnain. Ahead of me, I could see a cameraman with a very professional-looking cine camera set up on the top of the trig point. A well-known television personality was preparing to do some filming and commentary. I checked that it was okay to eat at the cairn so long as I kept quiet. The filming was going to be a 360 degree panorama so I was asked to keep my head down.

I asked which way they had come up that morning and there was a bit of an embarrassed silence. I had heard a helicopter earlier and asked if it was anything to do with them. They admitted that it was but emphasized that they had walked up the hill a couple of weeks earlier but that conditions had not been suitable for filming. Today's work had to be squeezed into the schedule. I later found the helicopter tucked under the south edge of the summit plateau a full 100 yards away from the filming!

I then watched some of the filming and commentary which developed into a bit of a pantomime. Walkers kept wandering into shot from various directions. Shouting from nearby would ruin the commentary. Occasionally, our personality would fluff her lines. I excused myself after the eighth take thinking that there was some good material there for It'll be alright on the night!

Trig Comings and Goings

I was one of a group who accompanied a friend when he was completing his Munros on Ben Vane. I was a bit surprised on the summit when he unpacked several items from his rucksack and proceeded to build a replica trig-point with cloth and rods. He explained that Ben Vane was the only Arrochar Alp without a trig and it deserved better. I hasten to add that, after our celebrations, he took all the pieces back down with him.

The Ben Vane New Trig

Photo Opportunity

Donald was teaching me the rudiments of rock-climbing and we had gone for the day to the Cobbler. We had gone up a couple of short routes on the North Peak and were now on a route that would bring us out just below the summit. It might have been Right-angled Gully but it was a long time ago and I cannot be sure. We had gone up the gully to where the crux of the direct finish was just above us. The doctor decided to take the easier line with his apprentice. This entailed traversing out to the right on a ledge, moving straight up for a few feet to a higher ledge which led back into the gully above the crux. Donald traversed to the end of the lower ledge and brought me over. It was only twenty or thirty feet from the top of the North Peak and we could hear the chattering of people up there. He then made a couple of moves straight up to the higher ledge and back across into the gully. He prepared the rope to take me in and called on me to climb. "By the way," he shouted, "this is one of these situations where the lead cannot fully protect you. If you fall, you will pendulum into the gully below me."

With that, several cameras peeped over from the summit.

Drowning in Arrochar

On another visit to the Cobbler, our physics teacher friend Iain had brought along an aneroid barometer from the school laboratory and, before we started up the hill, he carefully set it to the correct altitude. When we "threaded the needle" and were crowded together on the somewhat small summit, Iain consulted his barometer and announced that we had discovered a new Munro. He reset the instrument to the correct height of the Cobbler and we descended to a tea-room in Arrochar.

"I hope that you're all wearing your snorkels," he said. "We're now 120 feet under water."

The Wrong Dam

A group of my friends had been climbing in the Meall an Fhudair group of hills west of Glen Falloch. Their plan was to drop south to hit the Lairig Arnan for the walk back to their car at Inverarnan.

It was a very misty day but they navigated over their hill and aimed south to reach the side glen for the easy walk back to the car. They were, unfortunately, using a pre-war map which did not include all the hydro workings in the area. The reservoir on the Alt na Lairige above Glen Fyne appeared vaguely out of the mist ahead of them but, unknown to them, was not marked on their map. It was clearly a reservoir as they could see the usual shoreline scar. They were somewhat puzzled by this as the nearest stretch of dammed water on their map was Loch Sloy which at the time of their trip did not have the trees presently at its north end. After due deliberation they persuaded themselves that they must have been going well and it was, indeed, Loch Sloy. Accordingly, they decided that they would have to travel north-east to get back to their car. The high ground above them must be the slopes of Ben Vorlich so they would have to go slightly west of north to get round the north end of it and then swing north-east. Thus it was that, instead of moving north-east along Srath Dubh-uisage towards Glen Falloch as they thought, they were actually travelling north-east in the upper reaches of Glen Fyne.

After they had been travelling for some time, they reckoned that they should be reaching Glen Falloch but the terrain did not seem to fit. They could see a glen going off to the east and, whilst still completely lost although not totally aware of that, they made a logical decision which probably saved an overnighter in the hills. They turned east arguing that, so long as they did not hit a mountain barrier, they were bound to eventually hit Glen Falloch.

Thus, after a delay of several hours, they eventually emerged into the glen from Gleann nan Caorann and only had to walk a mile down the main-road to get back to their car. Nowadays, the GPS definitely has its advantages.

Central Gully in Quick-time

On a beautiful calm February day without a cloud in the sky, a party of us went in from Dalrigh past Cononish to climb the Central Gully of Ben Lui. It was one of these warm winter days where time seems to stand still and there is no pressure to rush.

The snow was hard-packed and we soon had crampons on and began a steady progress up the steepening slope. We passed a man edging down who informed us that he could not go on without crampons but that his properly equipped daughters were carrying on up. We could see them a couple of hundred feet above us. We slowly moved up on the girls and as we got nearer were astounded by what we saw. They were ascending roped together but level with each other on either side of the broad gully such that the rope stretched across it. Spare rope was loosely draped around their bodies. There were several parties coming up behind us and, if the girls slipped, they were liable to bring down about twenty people with them. We shouted a warning to

Beinn Lui and Central Gully

the climbers beneath us who were, like ourselves, unroped. At that, the gully became a heaving mass of humanity all racing to get to the relative sanctuary above the rope. The girls seemed to be blissfully unaware of the possible danger and looked on in amazement as everybody raced past.

What started as a leisurely ascent had become a sweaty stampede.

Dedication to the Hills

I was walking in the Crianlarich hills one Saturday and came upon two chaps going in the same direction as me. We walked along together and it transpired that they were from the north-east of England. They explained that they had almost completed the Munros this side of the Great Glen and would have to start making plans as to how to cope with the further away hills I could not believe their method of ticking off the hills to date. They would finish their work on Friday, go home for dinner and then go to their beds until after midnight. They would then drive to Scotland in the darkness and start on their next hills at dawn. I asked them if they camped or used hostels on the Saturday night and was astounded by the reply. They could only come to the hills at all so long as they were home to be with their families on the Sunday. They therefore drove home on Saturday evening stopping at a chip-shop on the way for some dinner.

Map Joins in Glen Lochay

It was a cloudless spring day and a couple of new Club members asked if I would take them somewhere local for a day out in the hills. I thought that Creag Mhòr and Beinn Heasgarnich would fit the bill so we went up to Killin and into Glen Lochay.

The two said that they were interested in Tops as well as Munros so I said that we would go up Creag Mhòr's southern Top, over the main peak and then do the big drop and re-ascent to Heasgarnich. Now, the ridges from Ben Challum, Cam Chreag, Stob nan Clach, Creag Mhòr and Heasgarnich drop down in a line across the head of Glen Lochay and, somewhat inconveniently, most of the tops are on one map and the feet on another.

We started off in clear weather where navigation was no problem and, chattering away, I led them up towards Stob nan Clach. We got to the cairn and I thought that the top was too flat and looked around. I had miscounted the ridges down in the glen and taken the party up to the summit of Creag Mhòr. My only consolation was that one of the chaps informed me that more military battles have been lost on the edges of maps than anywhere else.

Being newcomers to the game, the two were feeling a bit tired so we decided to forget about Heasgarnich. As we came off the hill, I remembered another time coming off the same hill. At the time, I was creating a rockery of white stones in my garden and near the summit I found a group of suitable quartz stones. I persuaded my two companions to take one each and we started off down the steep grassy gully at the south end of the ridge. It was hard work with the extra load so we scanned the hillside for humans or animals beneath us. It was clear. We rolled the three stones down and watched them bouncing higher and higher and disintegrating as they went. There was nothing to be found at the bottom. I did, however, find another source of suitable stones down in the glen. However, I was somewhat bluntly told that I had had my chances and there would be no more carrying.

Kilt Inversion

Three of us were having a short day out climbing Sgiach Chùil and Meall Glas in Glen Lochay. We started up the easterly of the two hills from near Lubchurran and were soon confronted by a high deer fence. Iain and Paul elected to divert over some pretty wet ground to a gate some distance away whilst I aimed for a nearby stout fence-post to climb the barrier.

I got to the top of the fence and, while standing on the second top strand, grasped the top one to ease myself over. It was absolutely slack and I proceeded to topple headfirst over the fence at which point my feet got caught in the top two wires with me hanging upside down. I'm told that, considering I was wearing the kilt, it was not a pretty sight. As I hung there wondering how to get out of this predicament, I got an upside down view of the others coming towards me whilst taking their sacks off and opening them on the run. I realized that they were almost certainly not thinking of rescuing me but were trying to dig their cameras out. With a superhuman effort, I got the weight off my feet and untangled them and re-inverted myself just before my 'friends' reached me. What the party from a church group who we met slightly further up the hill would have made of the episode hardly bears thinking about.

Some months later, when I told this tale to a stranger in a pub, he said "Dangerous things these kilts. I was with a chap in a kilt when we tried to cross a low electric fence. He ended up straddling it, jumping up and down and yelping like a dog." The thought of this brought tears to the eyes.

Rising Damp

It was a bright and dry day when three of us went up Glen Lochay and climbed Sgiath Chùil followed by Meall Glas. The day had become more overcast but still looked as though it would stay dry. I fancied going on a bit but the others were for going off the hill. We came to an arrangement. I would continue over the Corbett, Beinn nan Imirean, and Ben Challum and be picked up by them south of Tyndrum. I dropped off the west side of Meall Glas and, quarter of an hour later, the heavens opened. It lashed down but I was too far down the hill to try to chase the others back to the car. I had to go on as arranged. There were no mobiles in these days to allow plan changes and, anyway, I still don't use one on the hills. I believe, rightly or wrongly, in getting my own way out of a fix.

I went up and over the Corbett and down to Loch Chailein where the valley was badly flooded. By this time, I was absolutely drenched and the sodden kilt felt like a ton weight. I was in water up to my knees to avoid a big detour in going over to Challum. As I went over that hill and passed the gash between its two tops, I remembered a group ascent in whiteout conditions a couple of years before. We knew the gash was there somewhere. We looped all of our axes together and tied a person onto one end. He crawled slowly forward flinging snowballs to see if they landed just in front of him or somewhere out of sight below him. We eventually made it but it was a hairy few minutes. On this present occasion, by the time that I eventually got down to the meeting-point, I was shivering with the wet and cold and the others got me into the car without changing and we drove off with the heater going flat out.

We stopped off at the Drovers' Inn at Inverarnan where there was the usual big fire. I stood with my back to it to try and dry out. The others started laughing and pointed out that behind me there was an enormous cloud of steam rising from the kilt to the ceiling. It took several pints to get dry enough to go home!

Lost and Found

Kenny prided himself on being an all-round mountaineer who knew his hills well and had good navigation skills.

On a non-club weekend, Bill and I decided to go for a quick jaunt round the four Mairg hills in Glen Lyon. Over the years, access to this group of hills and the direction in which they can be traversed has been somewhat problematic. Because of this reputation, I used to 'phone in advance for clearance to go onto them and I never encountered any problem.

On this occasion, when we got there it was pea-souper weather but, other than a bit at the east end of the circuit, it is pretty well defined and there are bits and pieces of fence to guide you along various stretches. The vaguer terrain is between the first two hills at the east end so we decided to start at that end, get to the top of the first hill, and then navigate carefully to the second. The rest would be relatively straightforward.

We started up the well-defined ridge to the first hill. You can pick a name for it from at least three which have been proposed but I've always referred to it as Creag Mhòr. Well up the hill, two figures appeared out of the thick mist coming at right angles to us. Before he recognised us and could bite his lip, Kenny said "Do you know where we are?"

The Height of Nonsense

A German TV company was making a film on what it called idiosyncratic activities in Scotland. It was to be part of a series covering several countries in Europe. The film producer planned to have a segment on hill climbing in Scotland and approached The Munro Society to enquire as to whether we were willing to take part. We agreed and I was appointed as the contact to work with the film's producer. On discussion, it soon became apparent that hefty cameras and sound equipment would be involved so a hill with a good path on it would be preferable. We reduced the possibilities to Ben Lomond and Ben Lawers. In our discussions, I had mentioned that The Munro Society had almost completed an eight-year project to accurately measure about twenty hills which were within 3 or 4 metres either side of the boundary between Munros and Corbetts (914.4m). I mentioned that Ben Lawers was not in this group but it was within 16 feet of being a 4,000ft. mountain and there was an interesting story concerning its height. In 1878, a group of estate-workers built a 20-foot cairn (long since disappeared) on the top to raise its height to over 4,000ft. The film's producer immediately decided that Ben Lawers was the hill to film on and we would simulate a measuring of its height with our surveyors' sophisticated equipment.

The day for filming arrived and a small group from The Munro Society, including our surveyors, met up with the film crew at the site of the demolished Visitor Centre. The weather was not promising. I explained to the film crew that we would traverse Ben Ghlas to get to Ben Lawers. I mentioned the occasion when I was beaten back one winter on the summit of Ben Ghlas by a gale which was lifting lumps of ice which I had to dodge. It was very dangerous but these dangers would not arise on this occasion.

We started off in very overcast but dry conditions. With three cameras being involved and similar shots being taken many times, progress up the hill was painfully slow. It was also clear that the film crew was not really fit enough to keep up a steady pace and the weather was deteriorating. Drizzle had changed to heavy rain. We reached a flat area with a small outcrop of rock on it but we were only halfway up Ben Ghlas, the intervening Munro. The producer decided to do some final filming there before beating a retreat. We then all descended leaving the film crew well behind. By the time that they appeared back at the cars we had all changed into dry clothes. We were then informed that they would film a sequence of simulating measuring the height of Ben Lawers so we had to change back into sodden clothes.

We were subsequently given DVDs of the episode, all with German commentary or translation of what we had said. The final film definitely gave the impression that we had got to the summit of Ben Lawers and measured its height.

1.3 Tyndrum to Glen Coe

Easily reached from Central Scotland for a day out but necessitating a drive in darkness at both ends of a winter's day, this area has everything from wonderful loch views to hands-on rock stuff.

Cruachan under Attack

We had completed the Cruachan horseshoe from east to west and were returning to the dam to get back to our bikes to cycle down the hydro road. In the distance, on the other side of the dam we could see activity involving a group of people and what appeared to be old army-lorries.

As we started over the dam, a man ran towards us from the far end shouting that we must turn back. When he reached us, he told us that a comedy war-film was being made for television about a German soldier called Private Schulz. We could not cross the dam as filming was in progress. One of our number rather bravely informed him that we had enough trouble with stalkers and were not going to be denied – especially since we had won the War!

We went on our way over the dam to the accompaniment of furious glares but no bullets in the back.

Extreme Weather

Our Club used to make occasional use of a friend's cottage down Glen Orchy. On one visit there, we wakened up to lashing rain so decided after a late breakfast to go to the pub in Tyndrum. We spent quite a time there and the rain never eased off. When we returned and started to drive down Glen Orchy, we found that the Orchy had burst its banks and the road was flooded to quite a depth. We tried to sidle along a fence but it disappeared under the water so we had to go further up the hillside where we still had to get over raging side streams. We were only wearing shoes and mine never recovered from this.

On another occasion so much snow had fallen overnight that we could not get the car out of the field and onto the road which was itself deep with snow. We had to get home for work next day so decided that we would have to leave the car and get the evening train back to Glasgow. We packed up and walked up to the Bridge of Orchy Hotel thinking that someone would give us a lift to the station at Tyndrum. The main road was completely impassable and a train was stuck in the drifts near Bridge of Orchy station. However, we learnt that it was hoped to get a train up from Glasgow as far as Tyndrum later in the day after which it would return to Glasgow. We decided to go for it. The hotel was crowded with trapped people who had slept overnight on the floors or in the bunkhouse. The hotel owner, who knew us, was not happy at us trying to reach Tyndrum because the rumour was that there were twenty foot drifts along the road and the snowplough could not get through. However, he realised that we were determined to give it a try. He paraded us in front of all the trapped people and explained that we were very experienced climbers and would attempt to reach Tyndrum but no one must follow us as it would be a very dangerous journey. He made us sound like Hilary and Tenzing.

The drifts were bad but could mainly be rounded and we successfully got to Tyndrum and onto the train back to Glasgow. We later learnt that no one else had got out from Bridge of Orchy until the next day.

A Long Night

Our annual dinner was in a hotel on the way to Glen Coe. Because of the nature of the story, I feel that I should not be more specific. We had an excellent meal and settled down afterwards in the residents' lounge. After a while, the proprietor remarked that we were the quietest club he had ever met. We were only warming up!

Sometime after midnight, he said that he was retiring to bed. However, he gave me a crash course in making Harvey Wallbangers, set me up behind the bar and told me to charge everything at £1. At 2.30am, he appeared in his dressing-gown to ask if we were ever going to go to bed. It was well after 3am when the party broke up.

One of our number, who must remain nameless, was going to have to return home to work on the Sunday morning and so had an early breakfast. The rest of us started arriving in the dining-room just as he was leaving. We had been there for some time when someone remarked that he thought that he could see our friend's car still in the car-park. We went out to investigate. He was sitting in the car, with his head on the steering-wheel, fast asleep. This was, of course, long before the drink-driving laws.

Food on Credit

It had become a habit that, after a weekend away in the hills further north, we would pop into the Bridge of Orchy Hotel for a bar-meal on the way home. We had thus become pretty well-known there. On this particular occasion, we were eating when the chap at the next table began to speak to us. He was obviously a bit the worse for wear and he went on and on. We were too polite to be rude to him so, when he disappeared out to the toilet, we took our chance and fled.

A month later, we were back there again. The waitress, who we knew well, came up to us. "I know exactly what happened a month ago. You were trying to get away from that chap who was annoying you. However, here is your bill from that night." We all laughed as we realised what had happened.

I remembered another episode involving the hotel. I had driven up from home on a misty winter's day and only started the walk to Beinn Dòrain at lunch time. As I walked up and along the ridge towards the summit, I met several groups emerging out of the mist and descending. I got to the large cairn which is short of the summit after which the ground dips before rising to the top. In the misty conditions, the smaller cairn of the highest point could not be seen. Not a single set of foot-prints in the snow went beyond this first cairn. Having a pint in the hotel when I got down, I was tempted to announce that no one had reached the summit that day but why spoil a good day out?

Bum-slide Extraordinaire

We had finished the traverse from Beinn an Dothaidh to Beinn Dòrain above Bridge of Orchy. We could see the potential for a long bum-slide down the south-east corrie into Auch Gleann.

Many years before, Jimmy had had a motorcycle accident and he used a walking-stick in the hills. The bum-slide would clearly need an axe for control and, before we could say anything, Jimmy had chucked his stick down the slope and taken out his axe.

Off we went. It must be one of the longest uninterrupted slides that I have ever done and it had us down almost to the floor of the glen in jig time. When we stopped on the run-out at the bottom, Jimmy's stick was about ten feet away. We walked back to the car and retired to the Inverarnan for refreshment. Our breeches had got wet during the long slide so I stood with my back to the roaring fire to dry off. My backside felt sore. Inspection by the others informed me that I had rubbed through my breeches and underpants right to my skin.

Next morning, my posterior felt very tender and I could not sit down. I went to the doctor and, after he had examined me, said that his diagnosis of burns was just ahead of his second choice of frost-nip. He seemed to find it very amusing which is more than can be said for me!

Scree or Ski Runs

We'd come over Stob Ghabhar from Victoria Bridge on a day in late May in a year when the snows had disappeared early. We decided that there was plenty of time to drop to the Bealach Fuar-chathaidh and re-ascend to Clachlet before dropping into Coire Bà for the walk out.

It was a glorious, sweaty, shorts and T-shirt day and we toiled up the bone-dry slopes to the Clachlet cairn. When we got there, we were confronted by a chap with cross-country skis strapped to his rucksack. On commenting that he was being somewhat optimistic, he said that there had been plenty of snow at the same time the previous year. We left him scanning the horizon for a patch of snow.

On another occasion in the same area we were staying at Blackrock Cottage beside the White Corries ski-slopes and the ski season was in full swing. We decided to climb Meall a' Bhuiridh and then go over to Clachlet and Creise. The first part of the trip is quite a grind from the car-park to the plateau but we were not tempted to join the hordes of skiers going up on the chair-lift. As we were slogging up the slopes in very muggy conditions, a voice drifted down from a chair. "What's it like then on Cardiac Brae today?"

Climbing in the Dark

It was a glorious day and a group of us decided to climb Curved Ridge on The Buachaille. It is little more than a scramble and I was wearing the kilt. There were several parties on Rannoch Wall and at one point I stopped to take a photograph of the climbers. We were just under a slightly steeper bit of the ridge and, by the time that I had taken my photo, most of our party had surmounted this step and only Vincent was behind me. It was several years since I had been on Curved Ridge with the result that when I resumed climbing, with Vincent in close pursuit, I took the wrong line. A head looked over from above and told me to back-track a couple of moves and come up another way.

I reversed and Vincent gave a strangled cry from within the confines of my kilt. "Christ," he said, "the lights have gone out."

Cornice Capers

One evening in the Clachaig Inn in Glen Coe, I was standing beside a chap at the bar who was drinking beer as though it was about to go out of fashion. I mentioned that he seemed to be enjoying a good drink and he told me his tale.

That day, he had been on a gully climb with a friend in one of Bidean's corries and was in the lead when he reached the cornice. He wondered about tunnelling through and then decided that he could hack away at the edge and pull himself out and over. He made sure that his second was protecting him and started on the task. When he had taken a sizeable bite out of the cornice, he anchored his axes above the edge and heaved himself out to follow them. His hands shot out of his gloves and the slings of the tools and he performed a backward somersault out over his second who managed to hold his fall. On looking up, all that they could see sticking over the edge were the two tools with gloves still in the slings.

He was getting the beer he had thought that he would never sup again.

Legless on Bidean

A group of us had just got beyond the crux of a winter gully climb in Glen Coe. The remainder of the gully appeared to be straightforward so we unroped. I hung back with Alan, who had little winter experience, whilst the others disappeared onto the upper slopes of Stob Coire nan Lochan carrying the ropes. Just before the exit from the gully, although there was no cornice, there was a very awkward iced-up slab to surmount. The move was only about six or seven feet but there was scope for a very long slide with unthinkable consequences if it went wrong. Trusting to the crampons and axe, I got over the obstacle and waited for Alan to follow. He had one or two attempts but was not too confident in the ability of the axe and crampons to 'stick'. He eventually said that he would have to retreat. This presented a problem. I felt that I would have to see him safely down and the others wouldn't know what was happening. Also, to be honest, I was not too keen on reversing the move.

A winter Glencoe gully climb

I looked around and I was close to a large boulder. It was secure and I could reach over it and there was a good grip underneath its far side. I grasped the hold and told Alan to transfer his axe to his left hand and to start up the slab and then reach out with his right to my axe which I stretched out towards him. I then slowly pulled him in while he cramponed up the slab. He slumped down beside me and, when he had got his breath back, looked at me and said "If my wife had seen me there, she'd have cut my **** legs off." The rest of the day was uneventful.

Not You Again!

We had just topped the Forcan ridge on The Saddle in Kintail (I know that this story appears to be out of sequence but have patience) when we came upon a stranger above the notch as you go along towards the main summit. He was not sure which way to go and we advised him of the best route depending on his capabilities. We wandered together up to the main summit and then went on our separate ways.

Six weeks later, I got a phone call from someone who said he was about to finish his Munros and that he knew my brother, Bruce. He had asked him if he could accompany him on the Aonach Eagach as he was not sure of the route. Bruce was just about to go abroad but suggested that he try me. I was very happy to oblige and we arranged to meet at the Glen Etive road-end a couple of days later. This we did and I got out of the car. We total strangers stared at each other and then burst out laughing. Alan and I had already met on the summit of The Saddle.

We have maintained our friendship and I subsequently joined him on his last Munro on Mull a fortnight later. We also formed part of a group which walked the John Muir Trail in USA's Sierra Nevada Mountains (see chapter 7.2). He wrote the John Muir Trail Cicerone guide-book after that trip and our party figures prominently in its photographs.

Lying on the Aonach Eagach

I had come over Bidean nam Bian, Stob Coire Sgreamhach and Beinn Fhada in Glen Coe and descended out of the Lost Valley to the main road. On the most perfect of summer days with daylight guaranteed till nearly midnight, there was plenty of time to go back down the glen via the Aonach Eagach instead of amongst the petrol fumes. I was feeling really fit and shot up Am Bodach and along to the pinnacle section. The rock was beautifully warm and the scrambling was a delight.

Halfway along the pinnacles, I came up on a group of girls who were making heavy weather of a tricky bit. I was quite happy to hang back and have a rest but they asked me if I would go up first so that they could see the way to go. I said that I shouldn't lead the way as I was wearing the kilt and not best dressed to go up ahead of them. The girl who had been leading and was at the base of the chimney said that they promised not to look so I went on my way. When I was halfway up the girl shouted that she could see what I meant about the kilt. "You promised not to look," I shouted. "So I'm a liar," she replied.

Aonach Eagach's Twin Ridges

A party from our Club, not including myself I hasten to add, went to climb the Aonach Eagach on an overcast winter's day on which the tops were enveloped in thick clag. They climbed Am Bodach at the east end and made the tricky winter descent onto the ridge proper.

In the thick mist they made slow but steady progress past Meall Dearg, A.E. Robertson's final Munro, and on to the Crazy Pinnacles. Hard concentration was needed in the winter conditions and they went on and on and on. The pinnacled section seemed to be longer than expected but eventually they reached the lower slopes of Stob Coire Leith – or had they? It was steeper than they remembered and the first moves were definitely not a stroll. On closer inspection they realised that they had returned to Am Bodach. They had made the first recorded traverse of the twin ridges of the Aonach Eagach!

A Long Wait

One crisp winter's day, Bill and I had climbed up over Stob Coire nam Beith to the summit of Bidean. Conditions were very clear and, as we looked around, we could see over the Lost Valley to a group of people in the notch between Beinn Fhada and Stob Coire Sgreamhach. They weren't moving so we presumed that they were having lunch.

As Bill and I walked the ridge to Sgreamhach, we caught occasional glimpses of them. They seemed to be having an inordinately long meal-break. We topped Sgreamhach and turned to do the traverse along Beinn Fhada. We came to the top of the notch and carefully inched down. The party was still at the bottom. We asked them what they were doing as we had seen them there a good 40 minutes before. "We were waiting for someone to come along so that we could see how to climb out of here."

Glen Coe Snowplough

Three members of our Club were having a short winter day in Glen Coe. Two of them were going ice climbing and the third was going walking. They arranged a time for meeting back at the car at dusk. The walker got back to the car and there was no sign of the others. It was getting dark and he began to worry. An RAF mountain rescue team with helicopter was in the area on a training exercise and he approached them. He described where the climbers had been planning to go and asked if they could carry out a quick sweep search for them.

The climbers had found that the ice in Coire nan Lochan was not in good condition and the climb had taken far longer than they expected. When they reached the ridge in the fading daylight, they decided that it would be safer to descend into the Lost Valley. The helicopter was searching in Coire nan Lochan but eventually, in the darkness, it passed the mouth of the Lost Valley. The climbers spotted it in the distance and one asked the other what he thought the lights were. "It'll be a snowplough," was the reply.

The 'copter eventually saw them, realised that they were safe and reported this back to the walker down in the Glen. All ended well.

Piping and Steaming

I should emphasise in telling this tale, in case someone should recognise himself, it is intended to be a sincere compliment and in no way a criticism.

We were in the Clachaig Hotel in Glen Coe one evening and a ceilidh had been arranged in aid of the local Mountain Rescue team. The entertainment commenced with a piper, quite obviously from a military background, marching immaculately backwards and forwards across the dance-floor. When he had finished, he retired to the corner of the bar counter where he was regularly thanked with 'wee goldies'. Some three or four hours later, the proceedings were coming to a close and we, rather apprehensively, saw the piper preparing to round things off. He lurched to his starting point at the edge of the dance-floor and proceeded to play while working his way back and forth across the room with, to put it mildly, rather ungainly about-turns. During all of this, his pipe playing was as perfect as ever.

Things Go Bump in the Night

Our Club would periodically rent a two-storey building in Glencoe village. There were several bedrooms upstairs and the bathroom was at the head of the stairs. On this occasion we were spread around the various bedrooms and, in the middle of the night, we were all wakened up by a crash and what sounded like a cry. We all listened but it was followed by silence so, comparing notes in the morning, we had all turned over and gone back to sleep.

In the morning, Gordon appeared not looking his best. The story then came out. He had got up in the night to go to the toilet, had missed the bathroom door in the darkness and walked straight out into the stairwell. The bang and cry had been his fall down the stairs. He reckoned that he had been out cold for a time which explained the silence after the noise. He said that it was nothing to do with drink!

1.4 Fort William to Kingussie

Big rugged hills with good pubs and bunk-houses close at hand and fabulous views, weather permitting, from the western seaboard to the Cairngorms.

Mamores Memories

I have many memories of walking around the Mamores and two come to mind – one not quite so clearly as the other.

The first was on a very windy winter's day when we climbed from near Kinlochleven up towards Am Bodach. The wind was so strong when we reached the ridge that we had to lie down, plunge our ice axes into the snow, and hang onto them to avoid being bowled over. We had a shouted confab and beat a hasty retreat.

The second occasion was when my mate Bill and I, who have climbed all the Munros together, decided to attempt all the Mamores Munros and Tops in one trip. We were dropped off in Glen Nevis and picked up at Mamore Lodge above Kinlochleven. It was a successful but very hard trip and we retired to Bill's cottage in Glencoe village to celebrate with other members of our Club. I'm known for liking a glass of vodka and I announced that I would have a drink for each Munro topped that day. I fell asleep after 'the seventh Munro'.

Grey Corries Incidents

Paul and I were on a trip from Coire-choille near Spean Bridge to climb the Aonachs and then some of the Grey Corries. We left the car near the old hydro-electric scheme level-crossing and cycled along the forestry track towards the Aonachs. Paul had a puncture so we dumped his bike and shared shots on my bike to get nearer to the Aonachs. Paul had to turn back on Aonach Mòr because he had no crampons so he decided to cut across to the Grey Corries whilst I climbed over Aonach Mòr and Beag to join the Grey Corries. We met on the main ridge but Paul had had enough. I was going on further so we arranged that Paul would go down to my bike, cycle back to the car and then drive on the forestry track to pick up his bike and then wait for me at a pre-determined place. All worked well until I got to the meeting point. Paul was there in the car with my bike but not his own as he could not find it. Luckily, I had taken careful note of where we had dumped it so we collected it on the drive out.

On another occasion, I was climbing the Aonachs from Glen Nevis and, as it was a beautiful day, decided to take in the western end of the Grey Corries. The trouble was that, the further east that I walked on them, the further that I would be from my car. I met a chap coming the other way on Stob Choinnich Mòr. He told me that he had passed two young ladies who were walking to the east end of the hills about half an hour before. I decided to try to catch them and cadge a lift back to Glen Nevis. After a pretty sweaty chase along the Grey Corries, I caught up with them coming off the last hill. They were a couple of trainee doctors at the hospital in Fort William and they were happy to take me back to my car. It 'cost' me afternoon tea for three in Fort William.

Training for the Hills

Paul and Cathy had got vouchers for a two-for-the-price-of-one offer on ScotRail. They invited me to join them in going to Morgan's Den, the bunk-house at Corrour Station from where we would do the end of the Beinn Eibhinn range and the hills round Loch Ossian. Because they wanted to make best use of their vouchers, they were keen to take the train all the way from Glasgow. I tried, without success, to get someone to join us to share a two-for-one offer with me. I was resigned to paying the full fare of £18.

We arrived at Queen Street station at an ungodly hour in the morning and joined the queue at the ticket-office. I got served first and asked for a return to Corrour. After a delay, I was asked for £5. "No," I said, "I want a return." The clerk informed me that there was a special promotion of a return trip to anywhere on the West Highland line for a fiver. I could see Paul and Cathy putting away their vouchers as I paid up.

We journeyed up to Bridge of Orchy where several hill people joined the train and we remarked to them on the tremendous bargain. They obviously knew nothing about this and said that they had paid over £7 for the short return trip from Bridge of Orchy to Corrour. They complained to the guard who explained that ours was a special offer from Glasgow only. They were not happy bunnies.

A Slow Journey

I should emphasise that this story happened many years ago as I would not wish to get anyone into trouble.

We were staying near Bridge of Orchy and three of us decided to take the early morning train to Corrour and climb the three Munros round Loch Ossian. We were not sure of how much time that this would entail but we had to be finished in time to catch the evening train out. We started out from Bridge of Orchy station and, although we knew the train to have a speed restriction over Rannoch Moor, it trundled along painfully slowly. After Rannoch station it speeded up but we had lost half an hour of our available time before the evening train. We made it at the other end of the day but the return journey was a repeat of the outward journey. We asked at the Bridge of Orchy hotel what the problem was but no-one seemed to know.

Some weeks later I was having a pint at the Ballachullish Hotel and got chatting to a railwayman at the bar. I recounted the tale to him and asked him if he knew what it was about. "I should," he said, "because I was involved in the problem." He had been driving a goods train north and, as he pulled out of Bridge of Orchy station, unknown to him, a rail had broken and a wagon bogie jumped the track. With the speed restriction on that section and with plenty of power in hand, he had not noticed any drag. He had stopped at Rannoch to let a passenger train pass and, when he went to move off, the wheels spun and he could make no headway. Inspection showed the displaced bogie. Further inspection revealed that, between the two stations, the flanges of the wheels had chopped 60,000 fastening clips.

Engineers had replaced some to allow trains to cross the affected area very slowly while they filled in the gaps. Hence the severe speed restriction.

Horses and Drinks

Many years ago, I organised an office weekend outing to Fort William with the aim of climbing Ben Nevis if the weather was reasonable. Many of the participants were young and pretty fit although without much hill-walking experience. We wakened up on the Saturday morning to perfect weather but getting the slow-coaches ready took some time. It was mid-morning when we left the hostel to climb up to join the main pony track. We had ample supplies of beer spread around the company.

Most found the zig-zags up to the junction with the main path to be quite an effort. When we reached it at about 11.30, Jim, who looked somewhat unusual wearing a suit with a bottle of beer in one pocket and a tranny in the other, asked if he would be back down "for the first race at 2pm." On being told that this was impossible, he about-turned and made for the bookies. Most of the rest were struggling so we collected all the beer into one rucksack and stowed it behind a large boulder.

Some hours later we returned from the summit and stopped again at the junction. There were several people sunbathing at the spot as I went to retrieve the beer. As I opened the sack and the cans came out, we were being watched by a wide-eyed audience. "It's amazing what you can find in the hills if you look around," I remarked.

Contrasting Finishes

I was joining Jill on her last Munro on Sgùrr a' Mhaim in the Mamores. It was a glorious day and a large crowd ambled up towards Sgor an Iubhair, some via Stob Bàn and others up Coire a' Mhusgain. It was so calm that, as we walked along the Devil's Ridge, we were buzzed by a microlight. There was a lot of swimming in a lochan early in the walk and lots of sun-bathing all day. We enjoyed alcoholic refreshment and a singsong in the beautiful conditions at the summit.

Eight days later, I was back in the same area to celebrate Peter's completion just round the corner on Am Bodach. We were going to go round the Ring of Steall. At the car-park at the top of Glen Nevis, the weather looked iffy but stayed dry. The party had no sooner crossed the wire bridge near Steall when it started to rain and the wind started to blow. We donned waterproofs and battled along An Gearanach and An Garbhanach in deteriorating conditions with the temperature dropping rapidly in the wind. We got to the summit of Am Bodach in thick mist. A bottle of port was opened but people were more concerned about getting down out of this hell. Peter took lots of photographs as we all huddled behind each other and the cairn. The conditions were so bad that he subsequently found that he had no shots as the camera lens had misted right over.

We had a large meal in the evening and my little speech of congratulation did not go down too well when I contrasted that day with the one eight days before.

High Tide at Staoineag

Some of us had a three-day weekend and arranged to go into Ossian Youth Hostel on the Friday night. We would then climb over the Corbett Leum Uilleim to Staoineag bothy, staying there on the Saturday night. We would return to Ossian on the Sunday before taking the Monday morning train out. There were no Sunday trains in these days. Two others with less time available would walk in from Kinlochleven on the Saturday to join us at Staoineag. All went to plan and, on the Saturday, we arrived at the bothy and got a great

Between Loch Ossian and Staoineag bothy

fire going. We had brought plenty of coal with us. There was, as yet, no sign of Iain and Alan coming in from Kinlochleven. We did not envy them their journey as it had been raining heavily since lunch-time.

Late in the evening, the door burst open and in they came. Iain was absolutely drenched. When almost within sight of the bothy, they had come upon a raging stream. It did not look too deep. Iain inched across whilst Alan observed. Iain got within two strides of the far bank, stepped forward and disappeared up to his waist.

Alan went upstream for a short distance and found a bridge.

The Big Sleep

I will reveal no names in this story to avoid embarrassment. It concerns a Club member who had the reputation of going flat out at the start of the day and then running out of steam later. I called him Mr. Three Hours Man.

He and I drove to Fersit to climb the hills on the west side of Loch Treig. Although officially they are two Munros, they are really a twin-topped hill with a drop of less than 500 feet between them. It is quite normal, after climbing the two, to walk back out over the first one as it takes longer to walk round it.

As usual, my companion set off at a cracking pace and dragged me up to

Stob a' Choire Mheadhoin in hard winter conditions. We dropped into the intervening bealach and started up the slopes of Stob Coire Easain. He was flagging and I got to the top first. We returned together to the intervening dip where he said that he would stop to take a couple of photographs of the picturesque snow scenes. He would join me at the top of Mheadhoin.

I got back to the top and waited and waited and waited. Eventually after about twenty minutes, I started back down to look for him and found him struggling up. "What on earth happened?" I said. "I was so tired," he replied, "that I lay down in the snow for a rest and fell asleep."

Rob Roy MacGregor

I had phoned ahead to book into the Grey Corries Lodge in Roy Bridge. Doubt was expressed as to whether there was space but they said that they had one room left. I got there that evening and was puzzled to find the whole place deserted when I was taken to my room.

Later in the evening, I was supping a pint in the bar of the adjacent hotel when a stranger came up to me. "Are you the chap staying in the lodge?" he asked. When I confirmed this, he said not to worry that my car was trapped in the car-park by lorries as things would be sorted out shortly. It was the RAF Mountain Rescue Team down to provide radio communication for the annual Ben Nevis race. They insisted that I would have all my meals with them. That was my first meeting with Heavy Whalley, the team leader.

I had a great breakfast with them and, when they appeared back in the evening, was treated to a slap-up meal. They then informed me that they were going to a reception in Fort William and I was co-opted into the Royal Air Force so that I could join them.

What a night with endless supplies of drink. As usual, I was wearing the kilt and was introduced to all the dignitaries as "Rob Roy MacGregor and, by God, you should see his claymore."

The weekend had a tragic finish as the team wakened up next morning to the news that one of their Nimrods had crashed in Canada and there were no survivors.

Stob Bàn and the Lairig Leacach

Bill and I were in our phase of combining Corbett ascents with a second round of Munros. We walked into the Lairig Leacach from Coire-choille near Spean Bridge and climbed Cruach Innse and Sgùrr Innse. There was time to cross the lairig and climb Stob Bàn. Although it was winter, the first two hills had not needed axe or crampons but, halfway up Stob Bàn, it was clear that both were needed. It was early in the season and Bill had not brought his crampons. We came to an arrangement. We each used one of mine. It is remarkable how you can make do with one together with an axe when you are aware of the situation. It's a bit like driving a car on the gears when the brakes have failed. You operate accordingly. However, as we descended and met people coming up, we got some pretty dirty looks.

When we got to the bothy at the bottom of the hill, I told Bill of an experience that I once had there. I had come off the hill and was sitting on the doorstep of the bothy eating my lunch when a bunch of squaddies appeared up the lairig. Their instructor taught them how to use ropes to cross a river in safety and then came over to join me whilst the men practised over the stream in front of us.

"That chap over there is not taking much part in the exercise." I said. "I've given up on him," was the reply, "and I can't really blame the guy. He saw two notices pinned up back at base advertising outdoor courses. One was for walking and climbing and the other for swimming. He chose the walking one and has ended up here. He has since learnt that the other was for scuba-diving in the West Indies."

A Thirsty Rush

Bill and I had left the car at Fersit and walked over the hill-path to camp at Strathossian House. It was a glorious evening with unchanged weather next morning. We had a magnificent but tough day, climbing the two Munros to the south of Loch Ossian before doubling back to Ben Alder and Beinn Bheòil. We chatted to a chap as we were coming off Beinn Bheòil. He wanted a quick start the next morning so was not going to be stopping at Culra bothy as we were. He was going to camp out near the summit of Carn Dearg, the Munro right behind the bothy.

Next morning we were awakened before 5am by the sun streaming in the bothy window and were away by 5.30. We planned to walk the ridge from Carn Dearg to Beinn Eibhinn and its Tops before walking out to the car. As we left Carn Dearg, we met last night's acquaintance packing up his tent. His quick start was obviously slightly behind ours. The glorious weather was really whisking us along and I remarked that, if we accelerated a wee bit, we might just get to Spean Bridge Hotel before lunch-time closing at 2pm. As we progressed, it became obvious that it was going to be touch and go and we fairly raced the last bit to the car. We ran into the hotel at 1.55 and sat gasping at the bar.

"Any chance of getting two pints each and drinking a wee bit after supping up time?"

"Nae bother," said the barman. "We've got an all day licence now."

Passing Pitridh

We were staying at the Blackburn of Pattack hut which is sadly no more. Once before, I had taken the bike there and had a very dodgy time lifting the bike over an electric fence short of the bothy. On a misty day, a group of us decided to climb the three hills to the west of the bothy. We started up Geal Charn, or Mullach Coire an Iubhair as it was known in those days, and Bill and I, who were faster than the rest, soon pulled ahead and lost the others in the mist.

We reached the summit cairn but did not hang around for the others in the damp, chilly conditions, diverting further out west to take in Creag Pitridh. We then retraced our steps to pick up the old stalkers' path from below Geal Charn to the start of Beinn a' Chlachair's north-east ridge. As we got down towards the bealach under Beinn a' Chlachair, the visibility extended and we saw figures ahead of us. We overhauled them and found that it was the rest of our party. We asked them why they were skipping out Pitridh and they told us that they were on the way to it at the moment. We pointed out that we had already been there but that they had by-passed it, but they were not convinced until Loch a' Bhealaich Leamhain appeared out of the mist.

With that, one of the party turned to their leader, Donald, and said that he had told him further back that they should have swung to the right. "Well, you should have insisted," came the reply.

A Small Inconvenience

We were at Jock's Spot hut and had had a pretty wet day in the hills. The drying-room was crammed full of gear. Next morning was much better and a few of us decided to have a quick jaunt up Geal Charn from Garva Bridge. We rescued our gear from the drying-room. Now I am notorious for rather ill-treating my boots so that it is a standing joke that mine are always the scruffiest. I grabbed them and we were on our way. We got round to Garva

Bridge and started to prepare for the hill. Why were my boots so tight? I looked closely. They looked bad enough for mine but they were two sizes smaller. I had brought Wee Stewart's boots (I'm known as Big Stewart). It would have taken ages to go back and swap them and we already knew that Stewart was going to have a dossing day off the hill. Mad fool, I said that I would go up the hill in his boots. The uphill was not too bad but, when it came to the downhill with my toes pressing forward, the pain was terrible. I seriously considered walking down in my stocking soles.

I have never made that mistake again!

Pitridh Paddle

We had been climbing in the hills south of Loch Laggan and planned to finish at Luiblea to the north. It was during a very wet spell of weather and the day had been no better. It was a nose-to-the-compass day in thick mist. We got over Creag Pitridh and descended towards Lochan na h-Earba. We came out of the mist and could not believe what we were seeing below us. The loch had extended away up the glen to our left entailing an enormous detour in the wrong direction. However, where the estate track normally went round the south-west end of the loch, the bridge over the inlet was clear although the approaches on both sides were under water. We went down to investigate. The approaches to the bridge were lined with large boulders which were only about a foot under water. By hopping from boulder to boulder we managed to get across. Our boots were sodden anyway but the manoeuvre must have saved us nearly an hour's detour in fading light.

In the Doghouse

Kate's Dalmatian, Jay, had the obnoxious habit, to put it bluntly, of farting especially in a warm atmosphere. The Club was staying in Jock's Spot climbing hut between Newtonmore and Laggan. It was a cold night and we had the place thoroughly warmed up for the evening's imbibing and singsong. Jay, who was lying under the table, started to perform with the usual shouts of complaint. Kate tried some remedial action. After a time, the atmosphere improved and the ceilidh atmosphere continued. Later still, the atmosphere was again contaminated.

"Jay, for heaven's sake control yourself," someone cried.

"I took Jay out to the car an hour ago," was Kate's comment!

Highland Invasion

The location of this story must remain anonymous for reasons that will become apparent. I was staying for a week in a highland village whilst I climbed the surrounding hills. The village was in the back of beyond where nothing much ever seemed to happen. I visited the pub in the local hotel each night and after a few days was regarded as a regular who could stay on after hours.

One night, well after closing time, the publican's wife came through from the hotel and said that a police car was approaching with its blue light flashing. We were shepherded into a store containing two doors – one to the bar and the other into the hotel and were told that we were to immediately leave the building by which exit was whispered to us as the police entered. Whilst we waited, the locals helped themselves to crisps off the shelves but said that this was a regular occurrence and they always settled up.

After a few minutes the publican stuck his head round the door and said that it was clear to resume drinking. The police had paused in passing to say that they had been to the local railway station to deal with a bunch of Italian winos who had locked themselves in the waiting room and were causing a disturbance.

I looked around and thought that the majority of Scots had never found this place and was most impressed by the Italians' navigation.

Yorkshire Bitter

Tom, the warden at Ossian Youth Hostel was due to retire but so loved the area that he wanted to remain locally. At that time, the signalling on the main line over Rannoch Moor was being upgraded. There would be no need for a signalman at Corrour and his house was going to be put on the market. Tom decided to go to the sale, which was to be in Glasgow one afternoon, and see whether he might put in a bid.

He took the early morning train into Glasgow but had several hours to while away before the sale. He decided that a pint would not be out of order and, when he went into a pub, was delighted to see that they had his favourite on tap – Yorkshire Bitter. He enjoyed his pint and had a second one. He realised that it was time for lunch so accompanied his bar meal with another pint.

He was coming out of Glasgow on the evening train and said to himself, "What the hell did I come here for today?"

1.5 Around the Cairngorms

This area has big hills which have to be treated with great respect in adverse conditions because shelter is hard to come by up high. I do remember on one occasion on a very misty and wintry day, when crossing a flattish scoop near Cairn Lochan, I checked my compass about 2 minutes apart and, in that time, I had swung through nearly 180 degrees.

On the Firing Range

Bill and I had been camping up north and had been washed out and were driving home down the A9. We started to compare notes and realised that neither of us had climbed Beinn Dearg north of Blair Atholl. The weather had steadily improved from Inverness and, although it was getting a bit late to climb the hill that afternoon, we knew that there was a bothy under the hill. We got out the map and saw that there was a track from Old Blair to the bothy at Druim Dubh.

We parked at Old Blair, organised sacks for an overnighter and started up the track by the Banvie Burn. Ahead of us through the trees we could hear sporadic gunshot but it was not the stalking season so we did not think that we would upset the Duke!

We were going up the north bank of the burn and, as we reached a clearing, could see activity ahead on a bridge over to the far bank. As we walked towards the bridge, we realised that a clay pigeon shoot was taking place with the marksmen firing from the bridge towards our bank.

We hesitated, partly because we didn't want to upset the shoot but more because we were concerned for our own well-being. We were spotted and a shout came from the bridge and we thought that we were going to 'cop it'. However, an order to cease firing was given and we were signalled through and, as we passed, pleasant exchanges were made.

Respect an estate's activities and the majority of lairds and keepers are quite reasonable.

Navigation Problems

We were walking in reasonably clear conditions east of Glen Shee and one of the party was a bit tired and wanted to cut his day short. He was not too experienced and before parting company, we gave him a map and compass and ensured that he knew how to use them. We then went on our separate ways and several hours later our party got back to the cars. There was no sign of John so we went for a cup of tea in the café and then we scanned the hills without success. We had just started to climb back up when we met John walking out.

"What happened?" we said. "We left you with map and compass and you should have been back hours ago."

"Yes," replied John "but you didn't tell me where I was starting from."

On the Trail

We wanted a different approach to our normal route from Loch Muick to Lochnagar. We would go in by the track behind Balmoral. The Queen was in residence and, as we started up the track, we came to a booth with a policeman in it. He gave us a cheery wave and we went on our way. As we walked through the wood, we heard a movement behind us and turned to see a man in a suit coming out of the woods from the direction of the Castle. We nodded but there was no response so we carried on. He followed us about twenty yards behind. We got to the end of the wood and out into the open moor-land. We kept looking back surreptitiously and he watched us for about five minutes. He then disappeared back the way he had come.

Later in the day, on the summit plateau of the White Mounth, a pony and three men in army fatigues and armed with rifles appeared out of the mist and passed us without a word. I wondered whether humans were in more danger than stags that day.

Bike Problems

I had been up Mount Keen many times from Glen Esk in the south but never via Glen Tanar near Aboyne on Deeside. The opportunity came when we were camping at Braemar and Ian wanted to climb the hill and we both had bikes with us. Now, I'm afraid that my bike maintenance is very poor and, on this occasion, my neglect came home to roost. We cycled in to the base of the hill and started to pedal up the lower slopes of the track which passes close to the summit. I had not noticed anything amiss but, as I put extra pressure on the pedals, the chain-rings fell to pieces. I had been dropping the fixing bolts on the cycle in and now I was left with no gears and no way to deal with such a breakdown eight miles from the car. We decided to leave the problem till later and walked up the hill.

When we got back to the bikes, I suggested to Ian that he cycled out ahead to see whether he could get permission to bring in the car to rescue me. He had another, apparently rather far-fetched suggestion. There were only a few short uphills on the way out. He would cycle alongside me and, where it was necessary, would put his hand on my back and push me along. I was rather dubious about the likely success of this but it worked perfectly. There was, of course, no problem on the down-hills where I picked up as much speed as possible to help me on the next uphill. Ian helped me up a particular section and there was a long downhill ahead with another uphill beyond it. I would really have to get the momentum going. As I shot down the hill, I saw, to my horror, two people walking up the track with a dog off the leash. Ian and I were both screaming at them to get out of the way and at the last moment they ran to the side. I'm not sure where the dog went but it was not under my front wheel. As we shot past, I shouted out that the bike was broken but that must have been difficult to believe. I'm sure that we were summed up as inconsiderate louts.

Foreign Loos

My mate Bill was brought up in south-west Scotland but spent much of his early adult life in Yorkshire. North-east Scotland was a bit of an unknown to him. On one occasion we had been up Mount Keen and we stopped on the way home for a cuppa in a hotel in Edzell. At one point Bill went off in search of a toilet and came back moments later asking if I could help him. This had me somewhat puzzled as I followed him out to where he pointed at two doors and asked which he should use. They were labelled Loons and Quines!

Luibeg Lighthouse

On a very dark winter's night, after a lengthy spell in the Fife Arms, we drove to Linn of Dee and walked in to the old bothy at Luibeg next to Bob Scott's house. We had not been there before and, in the darkness, took some time to locate the building. It was bitterly cold and we bedded down almost at once. Incidentally, on a later occasion, it was so busy one weekend that Wee Stewart, who was last in, had to sleep on a climbing rope.

On this first visit, we had a great time in the hills and I remember listening to the Calcutta Cup on a set of earphones under my balaclava. As we came off the hill down into the glen, I lost reception with England leading 3-0 and it was two days before I discovered that Scotland had equalised in the last five minutes.

Back at the bothy it was still very cold so we got a great fire going and it was constantly fed with material from the nearby woods. This, together with ample supplies of food and drink, soon engendered the right conditions for a very loud and merry singsong which continued all evening. The heat was such that we were all stripped to the waist.

At about midnight, the door burst open and two chaps came in for the night. Remembering our problems in finding the bothy the night before, we asked them if they had had any trouble in finding the place. "It was easy," they said. "We could hear your singing from about a mile away and, when we came over the river, we could see the sparks pouring out of the chimney."

Cairngorm Weather Contrasts

One extremely stormy day, Bill and I went to ascend Cairn Lochan above the northern corries of Cairn Gorm. In the conditions, we decided to avoid the Fiacaill Coire an t-Sneachda ridge scramble and take the Fiacaill a' Choire Chais further to the east. This is just a stiff walk. In fact, we were very much sheltered from the south-west gale and reached the plateau with no difficulty although the last few feet to the large cairn were very hard into the teeth of the gale.

After a bite to eat, Bill stepped out from the shelter of the cairn and immediately somersaulted backwards past me. When we had sorted ourselves out, we ventured out onto the plateau. We battled over to the dip before Stob Coire an t-Sneachda and started up its slopes. We were constantly blown backwards and making little headway. We knew that, once we got halfway up the slope, the north edge of the plateau became craggy with virtually no means of escape in that direction. Accordingly after a shouted conversation at the tops of our voices, we dived into the shelter of the corrie and retreated.

Our sojourn on the plateau had occupied about 40 minutes. Two weeks later we did the trip in calm conditions and the same stretch took seven minutes.

On another occasion, we were camped high in Coire Raibeirt on the back of Cairn Gorm. We had had a glorious day going round Ben Macdui, Beinn Mheadhoin, Ben Bhreac and Beinn a' Chaorainn. As we finished a long and tiring day the weather was changing. We had our evening meal and settled down for the night. A gale blew up and got worse and worse. It was the middle of summer and we were only using the fly-sheet of a dome tent. Suddenly, we were looking at the stars as one half of the tent unpegged. We could hear tent-pegs pinging on the rocks. It was a bright moonlit night and I shouted to the others to hang onto the poles while I went out to retrieve the pegs and the situation. They still talk about the sight of me racing down the hillside in my Ys picking up tent-pegs.

Insanity at the Saddle

We had come up the first part of the Lairig an Laoigh from Glenmore Lodge and crossed over Bynack More and A' Choinneach to the Saddle, at the east end of Loch Avon. We had been in clear conditions with good snow cover underfoot but crampons had not been necessary. However, all day, the top third of Cairn Gorm had been in mist.

As we started up the steep, misty slopes from the Saddle, it quickly became obvious that crampons should now be put on. Suitably clad, we continued on and, well up the slope, two figures appeared out of the mist descending towards us. Those of you who know that area will realise that the two were walking into an area where sudden drops have to be avoided and it is very much cut off from anywhere.

As the young man and woman came down to us, we realised that they were not properly equipped for the hills. They were wearing denims and thin anorak tops and with trainers on their feet. We asked them where they were going and they said that they had just been to the summit of Cairn Gorm and were returning to the chair-lift. We pointed out that they were descending totally the wrong side of the mountain into a wilderness. They should come with us up and over the top and we would see them to the lift. They declined as they did not want to climb again and said that they would contour round the hill till they hit the lift. They could not be persuaded otherwise and disappeared off east in the mist. We had told them not to go west as they would end up above crags and a slip would prove fatal.

I pictured them going round and round the mountain top as they might well have been too high to meet the lift. However, no incidents reached the papers so all must have ended well. I've no doubt that if something had happened, the papers would have had another report about silly, irresponsible walkers.

No Tors on Beinn a' Bhuird

Ian was soon to be assessed for his Mountain Leadership summer qualification. He decided to practise his skills on a trip to Ben Avon, accompanied by Wee Stewart. They started out from the Old Brig o' Dee and walked in past the ruins of Slugain Lodge. It was a glorious day and, as they arrived at the bend in the Quoich Water, it was obvious that there would be little scope for navigation practice.

Under a cloudless sky, they walked on chatting away to each other as they sweated up the slopes. Eventually they got to the top of the broad ridge and, as they breasted the skyline, looked around in vain for the summit plateau tors. Things were not quite right. Over to the east was a large sprawling hill with plenty of tors on it. They had climbed Beinn a' Bhuird.

A week later, Ian passed the assessment at Glenmore Lodge.

A Celebratory Walk

A few years ago, I was finishing a round of Munros in the Cairngorms. My plan was to bike in towards Carn a' Mhaim and then to walk up the Lairig Ghru and climb to Braeriach. I could then come round the high ridge to my final hill, the Devil's Point. After that, it was then quite a quick descent and traverse round Carn a' Mhaim to the bike.

All went to plan and just as I reached the Braeriach cairn, a party of four appeared from the other direction. They had done the long crossing over the Moine Mhòr because, apparently, that was what a well-known TV personality had said to do in a program about Munros! Possibly, she forgot to say that the helicopter made it easier.

As we sat chatting, they brought out cans of wine and insisted that I join them in celebrating one of the party reaching 100 or 200 Munros on that hill. Having already determined that they were going round to the Devil's Point, I readily accepted but did not reveal my own forthcoming celebrations. Until the last moment before coming out, I had been going to be accompanied by members of our club and so was carrying a goodly supply of wine with me. In fact, because of the glorious weather, my mates had gone off to climb in the Garbh Choire over by Beinn a' Bhuird.

Anyway, two of my new-found friends turned for home and I walked round the ridge with the other two. When we topped the Devil's Point, I produced a two litre bottle of wine which we proceeded to consume between us. They then had a long way to backtrack to Glen Feshie whilst I just had the relatively short distance to get back to the bike. After the drink, the bike ride was a bit wobbly and I was glad to get back to the Muir of Inverey hut.

A month later I was in the Sligachan Hotel bar on Skye when I got a tap on the shoulder and turned round to face one of the strangers from the Devil's Point. "You've got a lot to answer for," he said. "It took us ages to stagger back to the car that day." After a pause he added, "Mind you, it's a grand way to climb the hills."

Some year's later I told this story at a Munro Society AGM and I was interrupted by one of the audience who told me that he was one of these two strangers.

Camp Fire

About a dozen of us were camping at Derry Lodge and the midges seemed worse than usual. To combat them, we set to and collected a large pile of brushwood and soon had a big fire going. A couple of girls at a nearby tent were also suffering and we invited them over to join us. However, they declined and got their own puny fire going.

In the morning, there was a large six or seven foot diameter scorched circle beside our tents whilst over by the girls' tent there was a similar circle which was barely two feet across. Our group was all having breakfast when a keeper drove by, reversed and stopped beside our tents. We were all hanging around as he strode past us, walked right over our scorched circle and up to the two girls beyond. He then proceeded to give them absolute hell for using his wood and damaging his ground. Having finished his tirade, he retraced his steps over our burnt ground, passed us without a word, got into his Land Rover and drove off.

Cairnwell Capers

In favourable weather conditions, The Cairnwell at the top of Glen Shee seems to be a very popular hill for hang-gliding. Now, I am probably going to be told that I am wrong but this seems to be the procedure so far as I can see. The car with male and female in it parks at the ski-centre and the man goes over to the chairlift queue with his folded up hang-glider whilst the female, wife or

On the summit of the Cairnwell

girlfriend, departs southwards in the car. She might go in the opposite direction depending on the wind direction. The man takes the chairlift to the top of The Cairnwell and proceeds to build the hang-glider. He then takes off, normally in the direction of the Spittal and the female is waiting there for him to land. He packs up the kit, loads it onto the car and is driven back to the ski-centre where the whole process is repeated.

It just seems to be a bit sexist to me but maybe I am jealous.

The Water-skiing Dog

We arrived at Ruigh-aiteachain in Glen Feshie one Friday evening and two cross-country skiers were already in residence. They told us that they had got a dressing down from a keeper for moving the deer from the bottom of the corrie up to the top as they had climbed the hill that morning. He apparently had the deer positioned ready to be shot on the Monday morning!

The next day, our party had a wander around the Carn Bàn Mòr plateau and late in the day we descended by the same corrie. A herd of deer descended ahead of us – probably the same ones that the skiers had chased up the hill the day before.

When we were down in the old Scots pines in the glen, the keeper appeared out of the trees dragging a puppy on a string behind him. He proceeded to rave and shout at us for moving the deer down the hill as he had had them positioned well up the corrie. Because of the torrent of abuse, it did not seem to be worth arguing with him so we let him get it out of his system. He was standing beside a stream about four feet wide and, when he had finished, he turned on his heels, hopped over the stream and went on his way.

It was most impressive watching the wee puppy water-skiing over the stream on its backside as it was dragged away.

Donald's Doss

It was going to be a frosty weekend at Ruigh-aiteachain bothy. We parked at Tolvah and started to make last-minute adjustments to our sacks and put boots on for the walk-in. Donald, who knew the bothy well, was away like a shot to grab a choice spot upstairs above the fireplace.

The rest of us walked along in the inky darkness never seeing Donald, got to the bothy, went through to the inner room and up the ladder to the sleeping quarters. The upper floor was pretty full already but there was no sign of Donald.

We got our sleeping-bags laid out and generally got ourselves sorted out. As it was late, we bedded down for the night straightaway. About twenty minutes later, Donald appeared.

"Where have you been?" we enquired. "Walked past the **** bothy in the dark and went halfway up the glen," was the reply.

Donald spent the night virtually hanging over the top of the ladder with a dirty cold draught for company. He got no sympathy next morning.

Money to Burn

On another occasion, we were again at Ruigh-aiteachain in a very cold winter spell. We had spent the day out in the hills and returned to the bothy with clothes to dry out and ourselves to warm up. While we prepared our evening meals a fire was lit and, by the time that we sat down on the floor to eat, we had a great blaze going.

We had a very traditional bothy evening with plenty of singing and drinking. Later on, when we were possibly not thinking so clearly due, of course, purely to the excess heat, Hugh decided to clear his pockets of a sticky Mars Bar wrapper from lunch-time on the hill. He threw it onto the fire and someone remarked that it almost looked like a fiver sticking to it. Hugh's hand shot into the fire and retrieved the remains of the wrapper. Sure enough, there was a somewhat damaged five pound note stuck to it.

Next day, we were shopping in Aviemore and Hugh had occasion to hand over the fiver. It was inspected very closely especially as Hugh looked slightly suspicious with one hairy wrist and one very smooth and red. However, it was accepted.

Synchronised Evacuation

We were camping one weekend at one of my favourite spots, Derry Lodge, in from Linn of Dee near Braemar. After a long day on the Saturday, the midges were bad and the six of us huddled on the footbridge over the Derry Burn to escape them. The Sunday started with mist almost down to the tents and the midges were just as bad. The forecast was for better weather later so we decided on a quick getaway to Beinn Bhreac and Beinn a' Chaorainn.

We started out in thick mist and part-way up Glen Derry someone decided that it was time to answer a call of nature. He disappeared into the deep heather and bracken and crouched out of sight. The other five of us thought that this was an opportune time to do likewise (in different locations of course). Moments later there was a performance of synchronised movement, if you'll pardon the expression, as six people all stood up simultaneously pulling their breeks up.

It turned out to be one of these marvellous days as, halfway up the first hill we walked out of the mist into a cloudless sky.

Revealing Ryvoan

We had had a long day in the Cairngorms, tramping for nearly thirty miles, and the evening of conviviality in Ryvoan bothy had done nothing to restore our energy. Someone looked out early next morning and announced that the weather was not very promising. We all settled deeper into our sacks until a ridiculously late hour. I'm never one to lie in so eventually got up and brewed a pot of tea. It was a mild morning and I had not got round to putting on any clothes so was dressed only in my overnight Ys. I was standing at the window drinking a mug of tea whilst surveying the world at large when the door burst open and a female walked in whilst looking back to a group of followers. "And this is a typical mountain bothy," she said as all eyes craned past her to my apparition beyond.

I hope that they were suitably impressed.

Potential Disasters

I remember two episodes around the Cairngorms where the casualness of youth could have led to disaster.

In the first, the wind was so strong that we reckoned that the high tops would be impossible so we hired cross-country skis. We skied up towards Gleann Einich but conditions were impossible beyond the top of the woods. We retreated and took the trail to Loch an Eilein. It was thick with ice and someone had the bright idea that we could ski across it. We opened our anoraks and used them as sails and got blown towards the middle at high speed. As we progressed we noticed that the top surface was getting very watery. We beat a hasty move towards the shore and then continued close to it round to the far side. As we shot up the shore and onto the path we got strange looks from the husky teams which were on their annual outing. It was the first time for many years that they were able to use sledges with skids as opposed to wheels.

The second incident occurred when I was recovering from a cycling accident where I came off second best with a lorry and broke eight ribs. Actually, my consultant said that it might have been more but other body parts concealed the other four from the x-ray. To answer my question as to how many were broken, he could only answer by doing a post-mortem! On my first day back in the hills after a long lay-off, two of us cycled in to Geldie Lodge to climb An Sgarsoch and Carn an Fhidhleir. It was a glorious day and on the cycle out on the excellent track our speed got higher and higher. I was still aching a bit from my injuries and wondered what the newspapers would make of it if I had another accident. However, all ended well.

Fife Arms Alarm

I have spent many an evening in the Fife Arms in Braemar when camping nearby. I once commented to the barman "You've been here for a good number of years." He gave me a long look and then said "So have you."

On one occasion in the middle of winter with deep snow everywhere, members of our Club had set up tents close to the village and retired to the Fife Arms for warmth and drink. Jim recognised his next-door neighbour at the bar and it turned out that he was up for a skiing weekend and was staying in the hotel. At closing time we were not especially looking forward to going back to freezing tents. Jim's neighbour said that we could stay on a bit longer as his guests.

We settled down with drinks in the end of the front hall not far from the main door. Sometime later, the fire alarm went off and, a few minutes later, the local volunteer firemen came rushing in as guests were coming down the stairs in dressing-gowns, some carrying cases or escorting children. They went out to stand at the designated meeting point. We saw no need to follow them. We were close to the front door, it was blowing a blizzard and we still had our drinks to finish. The firemen gave us passing glances but said nothing as they quickly identified it as being a false alarm. They brought the guests back in and we were left in peace to finish our drinks before returning to our tents.

35 years later, I met Jim's neighbour for the first time since that night and he reminded me of that occasion.

Nae Bother on Delnabo

In recent years, The Munro Society has held its annual dinner in Grantown-on-Spey. By this stage, I was concentrating on climbing Humps – hills that have a prominence of at least 100m. Two of these were on the Delnabo estate just outside Tomintoul. In two of the years I made a point of travelling up to the dinner by way of Deeside so that I could climb those hills. On each occasion, I sought the keeper who lived near the big house to ask his permission to park there after I had already come up a private drive. I do this whenever I can track down keepers because they normally react well to being asked and I have rarely been refused access. On both occasions the keeper not only allowed me access but directed me to take my car much closer to my hills on estate tracks.

I have always found that keepers react very well to being asked and, if the chosen hill is subject to stalking or grouse shooting on the day, will suggest alternatives on the estate.

1.6 Morvern to Glen Carron

The hills west of the Great Glen are my favourites although it can be an area of extreme weather conditions. It seems to specialise in cloud inversions and glories.

Rocking in the Hills

I was attending the annual dinner in Strontian of a group who were ticking off Marilyns and my last mainland one was in that area. These are the hills anywhere in the British Isles which have a minimum drop of 150m on all sides before the next higher ground. Some of the people at the meet accompanied me on this last Marilyn – Beinn Gaire. We got to the summit, which is topped by a large boulder and I was asked to stand on it for a photograph. When I did so, I was delighted to find that it rocked slightly. Another name for a rocking stone is a Logan stone. A conversation then took place between two of the photographers, one of whom must remain nameless.

"Peter, is that an old camera that uses film?"

"Yes."

"Are you not thinking of changing it for something modern?"

"No. Anyway, are you married?"

"Yes."

"Are you not thinking of trading in your wife for a new one?"

"Well, I actually did ten years ago."

End of conversation in gales of laughter.

Lunatics

After I had completed the Munros for the first time, I started on the Corbetts. I did not, however, give up on the bigger hills but if they were clagged in I would go for lower ones. Corbetts invariably had a better chance of clear visibility. On a New Year's Day of clear spells and squally hail showers, we looked at the Grey Corries and decided that we could do better. We went over the canal to go up Glen Loy to climb Meall a' Phubuill.

We got to the farm at the top of the glen, which by the way is now cut off by gates as I found when I went later to climb a nearby Graham. The weather was having one of its bad patches. We asked the farmer's wife if we could park our cars while we went up the hill. She looked at us, looked at the horizontal sleety hail and said "Sure, but yer aff yer heids!"

Up on the ridge in the teeth of the gale as Wee Stewart three times tried to force his way through a sheep gap in a dyke, I was inclined to agree.

The Landslide

We had had an exceedingly wet day climbing Meall na Teanga and Sron a' Choire Ghairbh on the west side of Loch Lochy. Although it was early January, there was no snow on the ground and the tops were sodden. The stalkers' path to Cam Bhealach was running like a river as the rain lashed down non-stop. We got back to the car, changed and started back for our chalet at Roy Bridge. We were all desperate for hot showers. We got back round to just beyond Letterfinlay and were stopped by a policeman. Behind him we could see a bank of mud and boulders right over the road and a stream running right across. We were less than ten miles from our accommodation.

"How did you get past the roadblock at Invergarry?" he asked.

"We've been climbing the hills over the loch and just rejoined the main-road back at Laggan."

"Oh!" he said. "Well I'm afraid that you will have to go round another way. There's been a landslide and the road is closed."

We consulted the map. The alternative meant going halfway up to Inverness, cutting over on minor roads to the A9 and coming south and west via Newtonmore. It was a journey of 123 miles. As we considered the situation, a police Land Rover came slowly past the slide. There was a hidden driveway at the landslide and the vehicle, although in quite deep water, managed to use it to get round the obstruction. I pointed out to the policeman that the alternative journey was enormous and that, as I had a diesel, the water should not be a problem. He consulted with his colleagues and agreed to let us try. With much bumping and splashing, we got through.

Two hours later, we were watching the early evening news. A further slide had wiped out the adjacent bridge and the road would be closed for some considerable period.

The Coal-man

One winter, three of us decided on a variation to the normal approach to Sgùrr nan Coireachan and Sgùrr Thuilm which is to go up Glen Finnan past Corryhully bothy. We would drive along Loch Arkaig side to Strathan and walk in to stay at Pean bothy and climb the hills from the north. Incidentally, I'm disappointed that my favourite road sign in Scotland has disappeared.

The cul-de-sac

Not far along the side road to its end at Strathan there is a cul-de-sac sign. What made it memorable was there used to be a plate fixed straight under the sign which said 18 miles.

The last time that we had been along by Loch Arkaig was to go to A' Chuil bothy in Glen Dessarry. A party of us had arrived late and we found two people in residence in one room. When we returned next evening after a day in the hills, there was an entry in the bothy book to say that they had been disturbed the night before by a herd of invading buffalo.

The old path from Strathan to Pean had, at that time at any rate, been overrun by new forestry plantations. There was, however, a new forestry road going part-way into Glen Pean higher up the hillside. We had been told that where it ended a new rough footpath was beginning to develop down to the bothy. We took in a small bag of coal with us as we knew that, other than the unsuitable new trees, there was virtually no wood near the bothy for a fire.

We parked the car and walked along the new forestry track into Glen Pean and found the cairn marking the start of the footpath down to the bothy. We were taking it in turns to carry the coal slung across the top of our rucksacks. There was a lot of soft, slippery snow on the ground and the path was very rough. We were working our way down with the help of head-torches and at one point when Wee Stewart was carrying the coal he slipped, gave a yell and fell off the path into a drainage ditch which was luckily dry.

The other two of us rather forgot about Stewart and leapt down to check that the bag had not burst. He was not very happy at our sense of priorities.

A Night Above Glen Dessarry

We had intended to walk in from Glen Dessarry to go over the Faith a' Chicheanais to Glen Kingie and thence down to Kinbreack bothy for the night. Next day, we would walk the ridge from Sgùrr Mòr to Sgùrr na Ciche. It was a glorious summer evening with a good forecast for the morrow so, on the spur of the moment when well up towards the bealach, we decided to bivvy out high on Sgùrr nan Coireachan. We found large boulders to sleep amongst not far beneath the summit and, after a night-cap, settled down to doss.

I wakened up at about two in the morning and was desperately thirsty but realised that, with our sudden change of plan, I had forgotten to fill my water-bottle before we climbed high. I therefore opened a can of beer and, miraculously, my four companions were suddenly awake and sharing it with me.

There was a funny milky effect in the darkness but we could not work out what we were seeing before we went back to sleep. We reawakened at daybreak and realised what the condition had been. We were above a temperature inversion and everything from a short distance below us was totally hidden in mist. We could easily identify all the tops from the Ben round to Skye and north up into Affric. However, the most memorable sight was just to our east. The mist level in Glen Kingie was considerably higher than that in Glen Dessarry. An enormous 'waterfall' of mist was slowly pouring out of Glen Kingie between An Eag and Sgùrr Cos na Breachd-laoidh. I have seen many temperature inversions over the years, frequently between the Great Glen and the western seaboard, but I have yet to see a repeat of the magnificent and

Mist-fall between Glen Kingie and Glen Dessarry

dramatic view on that occasion.

It was a glorious morning so we took our big sacks to the summit of Coireachan and dumped them. We then walked out to Sgùrr na Ciche in shorts and T-shirts with some food stuffed in our pockets. As we returned to our sacks, the mist beneath us was beginning to disperse. We picked up the sacks and walked east as far as Sgùrr Fhuarain before dropping down into Glen Kingie by which time the mist had disappeared and the glen was like an oven. After wading the river we reached Kinbreack bothy.

A group at the bothy greeted us and said that it was disappointing that the good weather had come so late in the day. One of their group had reacted badly to the ever-present midges and had to hide from them. As the bothy ground floor was stone, he had retired to the upper floor which was like a furnace under the blazing sun. I met him some weeks later and asked him what he had done. "In the evening, I walked west for a long way until I got the sea-breezes which kept the midges away."

Deer, Deer!

Peter and I had driven along the side of Loch Arkaig to park at the road-end at Strathan where I once asked the keeper if it was pronounced Strath'n or Strathaan. "It's Strawn," he said.

I was reminded of two other visits to that area. In the first, many years before, there had been a small furniture van parked outside Glendessarry Lodge. I got chatting to the owner who was Herr Schmitt from Germany who had bought the estate and was in the process of moving in. When I asked him how extensive the estate was, he pointed out the skyline all around us and told me that that was the boundary. Thirty years later I was coming out of Knoydart and there were several vehicles outside the Lodge. When I asked what was happening I was told that Herr Schmitt was retiring that weekend and this was a going-away party. I sought him out and said that I had met him on his first weekend thirty years before. He was interested to hear that but I was never offered any of the beer which was going the rounds.

On this present occasion, we had walked in and camped at an idyllic location up the glen from Carnoch. We wakened up in the morning to a cloudless sky and prepared for a long walk over Meall Buidhe, Ladhar Bheinn and back to our camp via Luinne Bheinn. Incidentally, having done it, I would not recommend it as a sensible way to climb the three hills in a oner. Anyway, our camp was on the edge of a dark pool on the other side of which was quite a high crag which dropped sheer into it. Peter had paddled out into the pool to brush his teeth and, as I watched, his brushing action slowly stopped and he stood transfixed in a crouched position. I wondered what had happened and looked to where his eyes were fixed. About six feet in front of him lying on the bottom and sharing his toothbrush water was the carcass of a deer which had clearly fallen straight off the crag. Peter retired to a stream to complete his ablutions.

This outing had a fortunate ending. After a successful trip, we walked out to Peter's car and loaded up the gear. We went to move off and the oil-light came on. The dipstick confirmed the worst and we were off the beaten track and almost twenty miles from the nearest garage at Spean Bridge. We were debating what to do when a car drove up and parked. A young lady stepped out and started unloading her gear.

"I don't suppose you have a can of oil you could sell us?"

"Yes," was the glorious reply.

Sweeping Up

It was towards the end of a beautiful day in Knoydart, where we had come over Luinne Bheinn and Meall Buidhe from Barrisdale and, after the long cross-country haul, were starting up the slopes of Ladhar Bheinn. As we got to the west end of the bumpy ridge above Coire Dhorrcail and started up the final long slope to the summit, we could hear lots of shouting above us and could see people moving backwards and forwards along the flat summit ridge.

Part-way up, we met a middle-aged couple descending who informed us in somewhat disapproving tones that the summit was "full of people who are drunk." We carried on up and could see people coming down in dribs and drabs towards us. When the first of them reached us, we asked what was going on and they told us that one of the party was finishing his Munros on the hill. As we met different members of the entourage, we kept asked if one of them was the person in question but they kept referring to someone behind them. Just before the east cairn, there is a small rock wall and when we reached it there was a person stuck part-way down it. He appeared to be somewhat the worse for wear and readily accepted our offer of help. It was easier to separate him from his rucksack and get them down the wall individually. When that was done, we helped him on with his sack and pointed him towards his mates who had all gone on.

As he got ready to go, we asked him why he was suffering the severe encumbrance of an upright Hoover strapped onto his sack. "Well," he said, "I'm sweeping up the last of the Munros today."

The Inverie Pub

A group from our club had walked in from Kinloch Hourn to Barrisdale on the Friday night, planning to climb the Knoydart hills over the weekend. Bill and I were also climbing Corbetts at that time so I had made arrangements for the two of us to stay in a B and B at Inverie on the Saturday night. We would leave our tents at Barrisdale and travel over the tops to spend the night at Inverie, returning by another route on the Sunday.

We reached Inverie in deteriorating weather and settled into our accommodation and were surprised to hear that there was a pub, (The Old Forge), in the village. This was in the days when the area was not so widely known. We had a very enjoyable evening drinking and watching World Cup football on the telly. We also got chatting with members of another climbing club who were staying in the village.

Our first Corbett on the Sunday return trip involved a bit of a detour so that these people from the other club were well ahead of us in going over Meall Buidhe to Luinne Bheinn. When they got there, they met members of our club who had come up from Barrisdale. They got chatting and it soon became obvious that both parties knew Bill and me.

You can imagine the reaction of our club members who had spent a pretty miserable wet evening in tents at Barrisdale when our new friends said, "Oh yes. We spent the evening with your friends watching the World Cup in the pub at Inverie."

On another occasion, I camped at Kinloch Hourn, intending to walk in to Barrisdale and the Knoydart hills the next day. It was pouring cats and dogs and I was not looking forward to an evening pinned down in the tent. I had bumped into Donald, the local keeper, several times over the years. He saw me putting up the tent and he invited me over to join him and his wife in their house for the evening. This is the sort of thing that can happen when you keep on good terms with keepers and stalkers and it was very much appreciated.

Sick and Wet

Four of us had walked to Barrisdale Bay to do the round of the three Munros in Knoydart the next day. It's a long day so Hugh and I retired to our tents early. The other two, who were sharing a tent but shall remain nameless, started on their weekend's drink supply and consumed the lot in one go. Naturally, their constitutions rebelled and they were out several times in the night bringing up the contents of their stomachs.

It was a bitterly cold night with snow on the ground and a very hard frost. When Hugh and I got up in the morning, the others were not for moving. The two of us climbed our three hills and got back in darkness. The others had managed one hill but had been severely handicapped by finding that, in the night, they had been sick into their boots which were left outside. The content of their stomachs were frozen solid in the boots and took some thawing out with the help of a Primus.

Next day, the other two wanted to do their missed hills so Hugh and I decided to walk out and climb Sgùrr a' Mhaoraich above Kinloch Hourn. This we did on a sunny day with the snow having melted to leave it very wet underfoot. We descended the hill towards the car and Hugh remarked that he had little sympathy for the others and they were responsible for their own downfall. We were literally ten yards above the road when Hugh slipped on the sodden turf and mud and tobogganed to the road on his backside. I remarked to him that he also was responsible for his own downfall.

I would not say that Hugh was in the least bit accident-prone but I do remember another occasion when he came a cropper. Together with Vincent, we came to a fast-flowing burn on the way in to Ben Starav. We realised that we should have crossed it by a bridge further downstream. Hugh started down the slabs at the edge, carrying Vincent's rucksack as well as his own. He slipped and aquaplaned down the slab into thigh-deep water. No sympathy. Vincent just yelled at him not to let his sack drop into the water.

Cool Beinn Sgritheall

A party from the Club made a mass assault on Beinn Sgritheall from a point two miles west of Arnisdale on the shore of Loch Hourn. It was a baking hot day and most of the party wanted to get down to the loch for a swim after the climb. Bill and I decided to go east and climb the two nearby Corbetts. We arranged to be picked up at Arnisdale later in the day. As we traversed out to the small bump on the east end of the Munro, a shepherd hailed us and asked if we would mind taking a looping course off the hill as it would help to drive his sheep towards him. This we did and then carried on with our trip and eventually dropped down into Arnisdale feeling absolutely wabbit in the heat. We still had some time to wait for our lift so went to the village shop to get lemonade and ice-cream. We had forgotten that it was Sunday and the shop was closed. I shouted to Bill who was approaching that we had had it because it was closed on the Sabbath. A voice from over the garden wall said "Not to people who help me out."

It was the shepherd from the hill and his wife ran the shop. We were sitting having refreshments with him in the garden when our somewhat envious lift arrived but there was no offer to our driver.

One good turn......

A Golden Day

I was spending a night in the bunkhouse at one of my favourite watering holes, the Tomdoun Hotel on Loch Garry. In the bar in the evening, I got talking to some hill-walkers who were staying in the hotel. They were very keen to climb Sgùrr Mòr on the south side of Loch Quoich. It is normally approached from Glen Dessarry along Loch Arkaig. I was happy to accompany them but it was going to be a long and slow car journey round to the start.

Now, at that time, the Tomdoun was very much a fisherman's pub and someone had the bright idea that we may be able to hire a boat to approach our hill from the north over Loch Quoich. We enquired and found that, not only could we hire a boat and outboard, but that the boats were actually beached near the dam on Loch Quoich.

Next day, four of us set sail from the east end of the loch and chugged along in excellent conditions to near the west end. The loch is of some length and the journey took us nearly two hours partly due to a refuelling exercise part-way along. We beached the boat near where one of the old stalkers' paths was marked as going up to near Sgùrr Beag. The paths in this area used to be centred on Kinlochquoich shooting lodge but everything changed when the loch level was raised for hydro purposes. Many of the paths disappear into the loch and we really felt that we were going back into history by using what must now be a rarely used one. We reached our target, Sgùrr Mòr, and then trekked west along the ridge over Sgùrr Beag and An Eag to Sgùrr nan Coireachan. We would have liked to have gone further to Garbh Chioch Mhòr but other factors had to be considered. The weather was turning black in the east; we still had a return sail of about two hours and there was a time-limit on meals at the hotel.

We descended a corrie to pick up our outward path and got back to the boat. During the return journey, the wind sprang up and rain swept in but luckily most of it bypassed us. Near the end of the journey, we had to refuel again and had some difficulty in restarting the outboard. My knowledge of how to deal with my temperamental Flymo at home came in handy and we got going again on the last half mile.

During the last few hundred yards, we were thrilled to be followed on the shoreline by a golden eagle which looked absolutely magnificent as its plumage glowed in the setting sun. What a way to end a most unusual hill-walking day.

That evening, I was talking to an old chap in a corner of the Tomdoun bar and he mentioned an intriguing fact. Loch Hourn is a long sea loch with a narrows halfway along it. He said that, in the old days, so many fishing boats used to lay up in the narrows you could cross from one shore to the other over the decks.

Saileag

I was on a solo trip down the north side of Glen Shiel from Cluanie Inn to the far end of the Five Sisters when I came upon a small party from Prestwick on Aonach Meadhoin. They were a young husband and wife with two friends. We walked on together over Sgùrr a' Bhealaich Dheirg with its cairn in a marvellous position just north of the main ridge.

Eventually, we came to the slopes of Saileag and, as we ascended, the wife commented to her husband that it was a beautiful name. The husband agreed and said that it would make a lovely girl's name and added, possibly with a hint of a twinkle in his eye, that it would be a great name for his wife. She gave a large appreciative smile and asked him if he had any idea what it meant.

"Yes," he said, "Little Heel."

Army Manoeuvres

Back in the eighties White Cottage beyond the road-end in Glen Affric was an open bothy. Regretfully, for hill folk it has apparently been turned into the retirement home for the previous landowner.

A group of us was in residence one weekend when, early on the Saturday morning, there was a loud knock at the door. Standing there was a gentleman dressed in army uniform. He told us that there were to be military exercises involving the Territorial Army. The first exercise would take place within the hour just beyond the cottage. We were not to be alarmed by the noise because they would only be using blanks.

A few minutes later, some army lorries deposited a large group of soldiers in a nearby flat area occupied, at the far side, by two white garrons (ponies) – it was just after the stalking season. The men were led over a bridge to

White Cottage and the garrons

the far side of a sizeable stream and spread over a hillock which they were to defend. It was an overcast day and we were in no rush to go up the hills so we wandered outside with our cups of tea to watch the proceedings. The empty lorries disappeared down the glen. About 20 minutes later the lorries reappeared and dropped off another load of men short of the cottage. They were organised across the level area and crawled forward under their sergeant-major's orders. Defence firing had just started from the hillock over the stream when the two ponies trotted up to see what was going on. To a man, the attacking force rose to its feet and ran away from the horses and straight across the thigh-deep stream despite cries to get down accompanied by the volley of firing from the far side.

I have maintained ever since that, instead of the nuclear deterrent, all the Russians need is a string of white horses. Now that I have read Hamish Brown's Foreword to this book, it seems that Highland coos would do just as well.

It's a Small World

I had had a day out in the hills above Glen Affric and had come off the last hill, Mullach na Dheiragain into Gleann a' Choilich to its east. My way home was then up and over the Bealach Coire Ghaidheil to the Alltbeithe path for the cycle out to the Affric car-park. As I climbed up the steep stalkers' path to the bealach, I overhauled an older person struggling up with a large load. We got chatting and it turned out that he was on the Ultimate Challenge, now the TGO Challenge, and his companions had gone up the slope ahead of him and were waiting at the top. I recognised his Angus accent and asked him where he came from. He replied, "Letham," which is just along the road from Kirriemuir where I was born and brought up. When I introduced myself he said that some years before his doctor's name had been Logan. It soon became apparent that he was talking about my father.

We got to the bealach where his companions had been joined by a girl who was also doing the Ultimate. I recounted the coincidence about my father and the girl said that she knew of a doctor of the same name but he was still practising in the West of Scotland. When she said where I was dumbfounded. That doctor and his wife, who are not related to us, are amongst our closest friends.

Long Memory

It was a beautiful evening at Alltbeithe Youth Hostel at the top of Glen Affric and, surprisingly, it was less than half full. On the instruction of the warden, who was a Polish student that year, we had done various chores and were now lying around outside enjoying the evening sun. A group of four hikers appeared from the Loch Affric direction and, from their accents and flags sewn onto their sacks, it was obvious that they were Germans. They found the warden and asked if there was any accommodation. "No." he said. "The hostel is full." They asked him where they might find accommodation and he directed them to Camban bothy two miles away or Ratagan hostel a good twelve miles down Gleann Lichd. At 7pm they proceeded on their way.

When they had got out of earshot, I said that I was surprised that there was no space in our hostel. "Not for them after what they did to my country in the War," he replied.

Camera Call

My old film camera was giving more and more problems. A lot of shots were turning out to be out of focus or overexposed when the slides were returned. The result was that I was tending to take each shot twice in the hope that one would be okay. This made for expensive photography. It's all changed nowadays, of course, with digital photography.

On one occasion we were doing a long route beyond the locked gate into

Glen Strathfarrar. There wasn't much time for hanging about as we had to be back out through the gate by a specific time. It was a lovely day and we got round the hills faster than I expected so we could sit in the sun outside the car for a bit. I went to take a photograph of the others and realised that I had left my camera on one of the summit cairns. Whilst we were still lounging about, another party came off the hill and came over to us. "Is this your camera?" one said. "We found it on the last top."

I was sorely tempted to say that I had never seen it before.

Isolation Shepherd

I had cycled in from Attadale to Bendronaig Lodge to climb Bidein a' Choire Sheasgaich and Lurg Mhòr. There was a Land Rover outside the bothy and a party of fishermen and a ghillie were having a brew-up before going up to Loch Calavie. They offered me a welcome cuppa and we got chatting. I remarked that they were fishing in a beautiful area and, having been here, they would enjoy reading Isolation Shepherd by Iain Thomson. He had been the shepherd over the hills on the side of Loch Monar before the area had been inundated by hydro workings.

The ghillie, who had been sitting quietly in the background, asked me if I remembered the Mackay brothers.

"Of course," I said.

"Then come into the next room. There's something I want to show you."

He led me through to a room where the walls were lined with old newspapers. They had signatures scrawled all over them. He pointed at one and said that it was that of one of the Mackays. I remarked that that was amazing after me just raising the subject of Isolation Shepherd. "I knew that the signature was there," he said, "because it's mine."

Navigating on Maoile Lunndaidh

On a wild winter's day, we had trudged from Gerry's Hostel up the glen past Glenuaig Lodge to climb Maoile Lunndaidh. I remembered on one occasion speaking to a geology student at the lodge who had been given permission to take his car there. The previous fortnight he had been given similar permission to come in from the east and take his car to Corrievuic beyond Scardroy Lodge. The bothies on either side of the bealach were five miles apart but he had had to drive 70 miles to get from one to the other.

Going up Maoile Lunndaidh, I was in the lead and was climbing with my nose stuck to the compass in virtually whiteout conditions. Despite two pairs of gloves, my fingers were still getting very cold holding the compass in the bitterly cold wind and I was very glad to eventually slump down at the cairn and gain some shelter.

We had a bite to eat and then took a bearing for Creag Toll a' Choin, the old demoted summit but which has subsequently been confirmed by Alan Dawson as the highest point. We knew that, in the conditions, we had to be very accurate with our navigation because, just short of the Creag, the two opposing corries come within a few yards of each other.

I felt like a rest from the lead to let my fingers recover and took out a Mars Bar as the others set off. I tagged on at the rear. They no doubt were thinking that a party can be adequately steered from the rear by shouted instructions to veer left or right.

After about ten minutes, the leader shouted back.

"Stewart, are we still on the right bearing?"

"I don't know," I said.

"You must," he said. "I can see you checking the bearing."

"No I'm not – I'm eating a Mars Bar."

We looked around us. The cornices were ten metres on either side of us. We had successfully navigated the hill by Mars Bar.

Ice Cold on Sgùrr Choinnich

We were up in Glen Carron to accompany Donald on the last Munro of his third round. It was to be Sgùrr Choinnich above Bealach Bhearnais in from Craig. Various parties were picking off Munros and Corbetts in the area but we arranged a time when we would congregate on top of his second-last hill, Sgùrr a' Chaorachain. We would go west en masse the short distance to the final hill with the views of the Matterhorn-shaped Bidein a' Choire Sheasgaich over to our left.

It was an absolute scorcher of a day in June and our wine was obviously going to be very warm. When we met on Chaorachain it turned out that there would be a delay whilst some people went out east to pick up the outlier of Bidean an Eoin Deirg. Whilst they did that and we were sunbathing at the cairn, someone pointed out the large snow-field just below the summit of Sgùrr Choinnich. A party of us was despatched ahead with the champagne and sparkling wine which we dug into the snow. By the time that Donald and the others came over half an hour later, we were able to offer them ice-cold drinks.

poles were so rotten that they could barely hold up the existing line let alone support a second one. He retired to report back and there was a considerable period of silence. The outcome was that the team down the road were now bringing in the solution in the form of an underground cable.

"God," I said, "that must be costing your boss a fortune."

"Not at all," he replied. "They've admitted that they have to stick to the price on the signed contract."

I wondered whether it might have been cheaper to put a mobile mast up the hillside and give them a free handset.

Missing the Maiden

One year in early spring we had stayed in Shenavall bothy on a Friday night and wakened to a beautiful, crisp morning. Bill and I decided that there was time to have a go at the round of the six Munros in the Fisherfield Forest beyond the Abhainn Strath na Sealga. They are six great hills but, thanks to a subsequent heighting exercise by The Munro Society, Beinn a' Chlaidheimh has since been reclassified as a Corbett. I've always called them the Fisherfields but they now seem to be known as the Big Six or even the Whitbreads after the name of the beer-making colonel who owned the estate at one time. The rest of our party decided to go for Ruadh Stac Mòr and A' Mhaighdean, the Maiden, returning by the path down by Fuar Loch Mòr.

Bill and I started out ahead of the others as we had a long day with darkness coming between seven and eight in the evening. It was our first time on these hills but we had no trouble finding our way past Ruadh Stac Beag and up and over Ruadh Stac Mòr. We saw, in passing, a small emergency enclosure that can just fit two people in the dip between this hill and A' Mhaighdean. There was extensive snow cover on the ground and the upper slopes of A' Mhaighdean were in mist. We got onto the summit plateau and went round in circles trying to find a cairn. Eventually, we persuaded ourselves that it must be totally buried under the snow so we took a bearing for our next objective, Beinn Tarsuinn.

Suddenly, out of the mist, the ground rose in front of us at the south end of the plateau. When we looked closely at the map we realised that there was an additional contour right under the A' of A' Mhaighdean. On the top of a small rise we found our cairn, congratulated ourselves, and went on our way.

We completed our round and got back to Shenavall at dusk to find that the others had eaten and were now into their drink. They remarked on how they had followed our footsteps up A' Mhaighdean and also gone round in circles on the plateau. They had come to the same conclusion as ourselves that the cairn was buried and they turned for home.

They were rather put off their drink when told that they had missed the top of the remotest Munro by a few feet. Over forty years later, one of that party has yet to get to the summit but he is now married with a family and appears to be confined to barracks.

On that same trip, Bill and I met a chap on Mullach Coire Mhic Fhearchair who complained that he had had to come all the way from the south of England to climb two new Tops on the hill!

Remote Meeting Places

One Easter, I was doing a solo clockwise circuit of the Big Six from south of Shenavall. It's a long way and I had started out quite early and the hills seemed to be deserted. As I came off Beinn Tarsuinn, I could see someone below me moving towards A' Mhaighdean. Hoping that he wouldn't mind company, I trotted down the hillside and came up on him halfway up the hill.

We got chatting and it turned out that he was a schoolteacher from England who managed to get away to the Scottish hills for one week each year at Easter. He had started out even earlier than me from the bothy, leaving his wife and children to carry out most of the luggage whilst he did the circuit.

We completed the round together and he waited for me at Shenavall whilst I packed my big sack and we then walked out together to the main-road at Corrie Hallie. We bade farewell at his camper-van and the meeting was soon out of my mind.

The following year at Easter, in good clear conditions, I was doing a solo round of the big three in Knoydart, finishing with Ladhar Bheinn. As I ascended the slopes of the last hill, I saw someone further up going in my direction. I accelerated to catch up and have a chat.

As I approached him, he turned round, looked long and hard at me and said "A' Mhaighdean last Easter." He was back again for his annual visit to Scotland. He only visited Scotland each year for a week at Easter and we had bumped into each other on two of the most remote Munros.

Weather Transformation

Although it was late April when Bill and I left a car at Kinlochewe, it was still very wintry with plenty of snow on the ground. We planned in two days to walk over Slioch, Beinn Làir and Beinn a' Chaisgein Mòr to Shenavall bothy where we would meet up with friends. Based there, we would spend a couple of days climbing the Big Six and Beinn Dearg Mòr and Bheag. We would then walk out to our car which would have been brought round to Corrie Hallie at Dundonnell. We started out with full loads and plastic boots in clear weather which started to deteriorate on the top of Slioch. We went over Beinn Làir in snow showers but the wind was getting up so we abandoned a planned diversion to Beinn Airigh Charr. We settled into Carnmore bothy for the night. We found enough material to keep a fire going for half the evening and then retired to our sacks because it was bitterly cold in the rising gale. A fantastic gust of wind hit the end of the building and blew the remnants of the fire right over us. I don't know if it's any better now but, in these days, the door was a propped up piece of corrugated iron and the chimney was a hole high up on the wall. You can guess, therefore, that we spent a pretty sleepless night there.

Plastic boots in scorching weather

Next day was still misty and wet although it was now very mild when we climbed our next hill on the way over to Shenavall.

We wakened on the third day to glorious sunshine and virtually no snow left. We clumped round the 19 miles of the Big Six in plastic boots. On the last day, we climbed Beinn Dearg Mòr and Bheag in trainers and stripped to the waist. In four days, we had gone from midwinter to summer. It makes you begin to believe the saying that, in Scotland, you can have four seasons before breakfast.

A Fisherman's Tail!

Fishermen appear to work to a different daily pattern as compared to hill people. Whereas in the main we are out in the daylight hours many fishermen seem to have a very late start to their day which can then drift well into the wee sma' hours.

On another visit to Shenavall, we walked in on the Friday evening with the intent of getting up early next day to do the round of the Big Six. There was a party of six fishermen in residence and we shared a fire with them until midnight. We then retired upstairs to get some sleep before the early rise. The fishermen started singing which in itself was irritating but not the end of the world. However, as the drink went down, the singing got louder and louder and things became ridiculous when they started banging the walls to the beat of the tunes. Wee Stewart lost his temper and went down to remonstrate with them. Apparently, one of them approached him in a threatening manner and Stewart pushed him away. In his drunken state, the fisherman staggered backwards and sat his tail-end in the fire. He quickly recovered but was very subdued. Stewart retired to his sack and there was no further noise from downstairs.

In the morning, the fishermen were sleeping it off but we were worried that they might take it out on our kit when we were out on the hills. We took most of our sleeping and cooking gear outside and hid it and went on our way not knowing what to expect on our return. As we left the last hill of the day, we met one of the fishermen's party who, it turned out, was more of a hill-walker. He was full of apologies as were the rest of his party when we got back to the bothy. That evening, we had a great evening with them and the subject of the night before was never raised. It was perhaps a trifle noisy but there were no other occupants to disturb.

A Sporting Success

We'd had a great day on An Teallach and after our evening meal in The Smiddy climbing hut, retired to the bar of the Dundonnell Hotel for the evening. Now my darts, to put it mildly, is not exactly sensational but I have found that my best play is when I have had three or four pints. Either side of that is normally rubbish. At the appropriate time, I approached the board and challenged the winner of the game in progress. When our game started, a girl was writing the scores down on a scrap of paper because there was no chalk for the blackboard. I played out of my skin and won and the girl came over and gave me the bit of paper.

"Och, I don't want that," I said. "Oh," she said. "You'll have to take it. You've just beaten the pub champion."

An Teallach Tragedy

On another occasion when the Club was staying in The Smiddy in Dundonnell there was a tragic accident – a double fatality on the Bad Step on An Teallach. We had seen the helicopter and the emergency services in the field opposite but did not know what was happening until we went along to the hotel. It later emerged that we had earlier met the party at the top of the Bad Step which we had just come up and they were about to go down. When we heard what had happened we realised that it would probably be reported on the late-night news bulletins so we rushed off to find telephones to phone home. It was in the days before mobiles.

I explained to Eleanor that there had been an accident but we had not been involved. "Och," she said. "I didn't really listen when you said where you were going so I would not have been worried."

On another pre-mobiles occasion, I heard a chap using the same phone and patiently explaining to his wife that he could not phone her next day from Shenavall.

Icebound on An Teallach

We were on a winter traverse of An Teallach and had safely made our way from Sàil Liath over the Corrag Bhuidhe pinnacled section to Sgùrr Fiona. The difficulties were now behind us – or so we thought. To make it a complete day, we decided to take in the outlying Tops and so we then turned left and went out to Sgùrr Creag an Eich. The wind had been steadily rising but the going was straightforward and we did not require crampons.

On returning towards the main ridge someone pointed out that we could save a re-ascent of Sgùrr Fiona by traversing over its north-west face to gain the col before the main summit. This we started to do and halfway across got partway onto a very icy section at the same time as the wind suddenly increased in strength. It was a steep slope and the wind was threatening to pull us off the hill. We desperately needed crampons on but it would have been foolhardy to try to put them on in the present situation. We therefore had to retreat very very carefully. One of our mates who had been well behind was still coming down the ridge-line to go out to the outlier. He was only about fifteen metres away but it took us the best part of ten minutes to reach him.

When we at last reached the sanctuary of the ridge, Wee Stewart said that we had been in the area where a man had been killed and his mate had had an epic going for help.

"Stewart," I said, "I'm glad you didn't tell me that over there."

Big Drop

Wee Stewart and I, together with Donald, walked into Gleann na Squaib from Inverlael near Ullapool. Donald planned to climb Penguin Gully on Beinn Dearg if it was in condition. Stewart and I were going to do the round of Eididh nan Clach Geala, Meall nan Ceapraichean and finishing with Beinn Dearg.

We parted company at the waterfalls but as Wee Stewart and I climbed the western ridge of our first hill we were able to see Donald enter the gully and make good progress up it. He was clearly going to be back at the car long before us.

Much later in the day we came to the bealach before the final climb to Beinn Dearg. Cona' Mheall was a "there and back" diversion to our left. We were not including it in our walk on this occasion but I was reminded of another occasion when I stood at this same spot. It had been in the middle of winter and the deep snow was very soft. There was a group of four people standing there and, as I was by myself, I suggested that we could share the trail-blazing in going out to Cona' Mheall. However, they told me that, in these hard conditions, they were going to give the hill a miss. I fought my way out there and had just started to return when I met the group coming towards me in my tracks. At least they apologised for making use of my efforts.

On the present occasion, we climbed Beinn Dearg and then started down its north-west ridge beside the six or seven foot high stone dyke that runs along the edge of the cliffs. We were keen to get down into the glen and over the river as far up the glen as possible as the river was running high with snow-melt and might pose a problem. Accordingly, we were looking for the Fool's Pass, a relatively safe descent route between the crags. This necessitated frequently clambering up onto the wall and looking for the right descent point on the other side. On one of these forays, we spotted a line of footprints going right to the edge of the snow where we knew, from observation from the other side of the glen earlier in the day, that there were massive cornices. The footsteps then came back to the wall. We recognised them as Donald's because the imprints showed a gaiter strap to be missing. We eventually found the descent route and sometime later got back to the car where Donald was waiting.

"Hey," we said. "That move to the edge of the cornice on Dearg was a bit risky, wasn't it?"

"Christ," he replied. "You saw it did you? I was creeping forward to see if I was above the Fool's Pass and was still about twenty feet from the edge when I heard a thump and a crack appeared under my feet. I jumped backwards and the whole lot just collapsed and went crashing to the bottom."

Ever since, I have always treated cornices with the greatest of respect.

A Bottomless Pit

We went up from Inverlael to do a winter climb of Inverlael Gully. Donald was leading as the smooth rock walls closed in towards us as we cramponed up the snow and ice. Suddenly Donald shouted down that we could not go any further and he swapped places to let me see why. We were on an icy pinnacle which tapered away to nothing about six feet out from the back of the gully. There was a very deep uninviting hole in the gap. We retreated!

Glory Be

I was staying for the New Year period at a cottage in Ullapool with Hamish and a group of his friends. On New Year's Day, eight of us decided to drive up the road to Knockan Rock to climb Cùl Mòr. It was a beautiful day and we revelled in the conditions with the beautiful views which Coigach and Assynt have to offer. The walk was straightforward with sporting ice which brought out the axes on the final slopes. There was slight mist coming and going on the summit and, with the wonderfully sunny conditions, I remarked that they were ideal conditions to see a glory or Brocken spectre. Some of the party were unfamiliar with glories so I explained that, in the right conditions of sun and mist, a shadow of oneself surrounded by a circular rainbow could be cast on the mist if the sun was on the other side of you. I remarked that it was pretty uncommon and that I had experienced it no more than a handful of times. This phenomenon was unknown to them so I said that you had to be on the edge of a drop so that your shadow cast by the sun would appear on the lower mist. I walked to the edge of the small summit plateau to illustrate where you would have to stand and, with a cry, shouted that there was a glory right in front of me. The group surged forward and I think were quite impressed at my organising the demonstration. It is experiences like that that can turn a relatively ordinary day (although Coigach is never ordinary) into a special one.

We had an alarming experience on the descent. One of our party had turned back before the summit and, when we got back to the cars, there was no sign of him. It was beginning to get dark so we went back up the hill shouting out his name. Eventually, although we were now using head-torches, it was pitch black so we retreated to the cars. He was standing there waiting. He had got lost coming off the hill and was far enough away that he never heard our shouts. Even if we had had mobiles, I doubt if we could have got a signal there.

No Secrets Left

A group of us was staying in a club hut north of Ullapool. It was an absolutely glorious summer's day and we decided that it was ideal for a climb of that wee gem, Stac Pollaidh. The sizeable party climbed by the path which goes round the back of the east end and we stopped up on the ridge to picnic and view the magnificent scenery. Some of us decided to traverse west amongst the pinnacles to the summit at the west end. Just before you reach it there is a very awkward move up a nose. This used to be relatively easily surmounted but the rock is now polished by hundreds, if not thousands, of passing boots and is considerably harder. However, slightly down a gully to the left (south) is an exposed groove which bypasses the nose. Several of us took this route and got to the summit whilst others watched us.

Now, I was wearing the kilt which was no bother in climbing the groove. However, on the slithery descent the kilt ended up around my waist. I'm told that it was not a pretty sight but it did not put off one person from taking a photo of me at that point.

A Flat Tale

When my family was young, we had a touring caravan and a couple of times a year I would take it up north to the more remote hills. It had an unusual tyre size so I always lugged around a spare wheel and suitable jack. They had remained unused for about seven years. On this particular trip, Bill and Donald were with me.

We had climbed Ben Loyal and were going along the north coast to Ben Hope when we had a caravan puncture near Tongue. Rather smugly, I changed the wheel. We picked off hills round the north-west corner and, a few days later, were driving down Loch Shin towards Lairg when the other tyre went. There had been no opportunity up there to get the first tyre repaired so we were now stuck. To add to our problems, we were getting buffeted by a strong wind.

We limped into a passing place and took the weight off the flat and put a pile of boulders under the axle. The caravan was rocking so much that we took a climbing rope, threaded it through two windows and tied it to the passing-place sign. Next morning, we took the wheel with the flat off, left the caravan and drove down to the garage at Lairg with it and the other flat. The two tyres were irreparable but they did not have that size of tyre. However, they promised to have a couple up from Edinburgh next morning. We were sceptical (look where Lairg is) but did not have much choice. We returned to the caravan and spent the day reading and watching the water coming out of a hydro discharge pipe high above Loch Shin. The water was doubling back over the pipe outlet, so strong was the wind.

We went back to the garage next morning. They had our tyres and they were already fitted to the wheels. It was great service and it's disappointing to see that the garage is no longer there.

Camera and Cairn

One of our Club members, Ian, was doing an ascent of Ben Hope from the south. The route on the upper hill is marked by a series of small cairns through the scree. As you breast the ridge, there is a larger cairn presumably intended as a return guide from the summit trig-point which is some way further on.

It was a very misty day and when Ian reached the larger cairn he was confronted by a man with a camcorder set up on a tripod. Ian remarked that it wasn't really the weather to be filming. However, the man told him that he was waiting to take a shot of his mate who was making this his first hill in an attempt to run round all the Munros.

Ian pointed out that this was not the actual summit which was still some way further on. The man thanked him and dismantled his kit and started to move on to the true summit. His mate appeared out of the mist and jogged past the cameraman. When Ian joined them shortly afterwards at the actual summit, they did not appear to be speaking to each other.

Behave yourself

On one occasion when we had a weekend climbing some of the northern hills, we wakened up on the Sunday to a terrible day of high winds and non-stop rain. We decided to give the hills a miss and drive home. We packed up and struck the tents and got ready to leave. I decided to send my wife, Eleanor, a message but I must have mistyped one of the words and predictive text on the mobile corrected it for me without me noticing. The intended message was "I'll be home tonight."

When I got home, Eleanor shoved her phone in my face and asked me to explain myself. The message received said "I'll be good tonight."

1.8 The Islands

There is nothing else like the Cuillin to challenge hill-walkers in the British Isles but the other islands also have much to offer. Personally, I find that four or five days at a time in the Cuillin is enough because by then scrambling on the gabbro has removed my fingertips.

The Cuillin Ridge

I have never done the Cuillin ridge in one trip and the one attempt at doing it failed for farcical reasons when it should have been straightforward.

We were staying at the Coruisk Hut and had already had quite a strenuous day on the Dubhs ridge. We planned to have an easy day when the weather forecast was not encouraging. We would then attempt the whole ridge the next day when the forecast was for excellent weather. We decided on this easy day that we would go up to Bidein Druim nan Ramh to determine the route over it. We were unfamiliar with that part of the ridge which is under 3,000ft. Despite the poorer forecast that day, the weather was brilliant and very hot. We got carried away and traversed the whole ridge from Bidein to Sgùrr nan Gillean at the north end.

Next day we were away from the hut at 0530 to go out to Gars Bheinn south of Sgùrr nan Eag at the south end. From there, we traversed the ridge in blistering heat as far as where we had hit it on Bidein the day before. Exhaustion had overcome us after three days in the heat so at 4pm we retired to the hut.

We thus did the whole traverse in two days but it was probably harder than doing it in a oner with an overnight stop on the ridge, because we had returned to the hut in between.

The In Pinn First Time

Like many, I'm sure, I was a bit apprehensive before my first visit to The Inaccessible Pinnacle. I was not in these days in a climbing club so I went with a climbing colleague from work. He was friendly with Ginger, an artist, who lived in Plockton in these days and we diverted to visit him and his wife. They kindly offered to put us up for the night so that evening we went round to the pub. Ginger led the way into the first pub and, before I could get over the thresh-hold, he recoiled saying “Christ, the yellow welly brigade.” It was full of sailors off yachts. It was another ten years before I saw the inside of that pub and then discovered its magnificent Bull's Blood.

Next day, we sailed over to Skye and drove down to the campsite at Glen Brittle. When we got up to the In Pinn, it was in thick mist which probably made things easier for me as we went up the somewhat exposed long side. When I was back down on ground-level, and feeling rather pleased with myself, Brian asked if I fancied going further south on the ridge. He wanted to recce it for a Cuillin traverse later in the year. I had so enjoyed the scramble that I readily agreed. All was going well until we came to a rather sharp drop, the Thearlaich-Dubh Gap, which was unknown to me. He saw my face and said that he did not want to put me off by mentioning it earlier. Anyway, I huffed and puffed my way over it to discover that, as you climb out, you actually end up on a pinnacle.

First time up the In Pinn (1979)

We safely traversed everything to Sgurr nan Eag but I think that the Gap stuck in my mind far more than the In Pinn.

Meeting the Neighbours

It was a glorious day on the Cuillin and we had traversed the ridge from Sgùrr nan Eag to Mhic Coinnich. There was still plenty of time so we decided to go as far as Mhadaidh taking in the In Pinn on the way.

We had brought harnesses in case we got this far on the ridge but were relying on cadging the use of someone's rope to abseil off the Pinn. Accordingly, it was a free climb up the long edge with much conversation to keep our minds off the drop. When we got to the chock-stone I was astounded to find Bill and Christine, my next-door neighbours, waiting to descend. I hadn't even known that they were away from home that weekend.

I mentioned to Christine that I didn't think she normally got into climbing and scrambling. She said that she didn't and was waiting for her first lesson in abseiling. I can think of easier first abseils but apparently it had been decided that nothing should put her off the Pinn before she got there.

She abbed off with whoops and leaps as though she had been doing it for all of her life.

Confusion on the Cuillin

We had just abseiled off the In Pinn, and were slithering down the loose scree on the descent from Sgùrr Dearg on our way to Sgùrr na Banachdaich, when we met two chaps coming up towards us. We got chatting and asked them what their plans were for the rest of the day. The said that, once they had climbed Banachdaich, they would probably turn south and go along the ridge to Sgùrr Dearg. We were a bit puzzled by this comment and asked them where they thought they were.

"Ascending Sgùrr na Banachdaich from the north-east corner of Coire na Banachdich." They took some persuading that they were actually climbing out of the south-east corner of the corrie to Sgùrr Dearg.

We went on our way and next day did the bit of the ridge from Bruach na Frithe to Sgùrr nan Gillean. When we topped the west ridge of Gillean, we found a sizeable group of people sunbathing at the summit cairn. They included the two wanderers from yesterday.

Tongue in cheek, I said to them "Well, this is definitely Am Bàsteir."

"Oh no it's not," came a chorus from around the cairn.

In Pinn Revelations

One of the few Munros that I had never topped whilst wearing the kilt was the notorious Inaccessible Pinnacle. The kilt is excellent in chilly weather but is a drawback if it is raining, as it has been known to do in the Cuillin, because, although warm when sodden, it gets very heavy. The chance to wear it to the top came on a beautiful, still day in late May.

We ascended by the west ridge of Sgùrr Dearg and it was obvious that on a day like this the hill, together presumably with the In Pinn, was going to be very busy. The masses were already gathering when we arrived at the summit of Sgùrr Dearg.

We rushed round to the base of the long edge before the queues started and, without wasting time getting roped up, stuffed climbing harnesses inside our shirts and started up. We were soon at the top and ready to abseil off. We'd taken a rope up but someone already there was giving free rides on his. I fleetingly thought about a classic abseil but decided that that and a kilt might be a very painful combination. However, it was quickly obvious that harness and kilt are not a good combination. I eventually managed to get the harness and figure of eight on and with bits of kilt hanging out everywhere, clipped on and prepared to descend.

As I stepped over the edge, a voice drifted up from the gallery below. "Ladies, avert your eyes."

Campfire at the Slig

We were camped beside the Sligachan Hotel on Skye and at breakfast time had just paid our camp fees. A short time later, I was standing outside my tent drinking a cup of tea when I noticed a strange glow inside a dome tent just a few feet away. Suddenly the top of the tent burst into flames which started to work their way down the sides. After a few seconds, a man did a somersault out of the tent which continued to blaze. We learnt later that he had had an accident whilst changing the stove gas cylinder inside his tent whilst he already had a gas light lit. He definitely learned a lesson.

Several of us ran over and concentrated mainly on the man who was trying to pull off lycra trousers which had melted onto his legs which were quite badly burned. We stopped him doing that and his mates then started to prepare to take him to hospital. The rest of us tried to save some of his items from within the tent which by now had burnt almost to the ground.

Suddenly a small dog shot out of the remains of the tent with smoke coming from around its backside. It shot across the campsite and sat down in a stream which seemed to be eminently sensible.

It occurred to me that we had better inform the chap who had been collecting the site fees. I sought him out and told him the story. He asked where it had happened and when I pointed out the location to him he said that that was all right as he had got his fee!

The tent must have burnt out in less than two minutes and we were most amused when we saw a sign at the Glen Brittle campsite as we passed through to Coire Làgan a short time later. It gave the Portree fire-station number to phone in the event of fire.

The Water Mug

Jim is a very helpful character but people can take advantage of this. We'd arrived at Elgol one evening prior to sailing in next morning on a pre-booked boat to the climbing hut at Coruisk. That evening we were going to sleep in the gents' toilet-block but it was rather smelly. The ladies' toilet was far cleaner and unlikely to be used after midnight. Our timing was perfect. Just after we got our sleeping-bags laid out and had got into them, a timer put the lights out.

Next day, we sailed in. Close to the hut is the river, reputed to be the shortest in Scotland. In normal conditions it spreads itself very shallowly over slabs and there are stepping-stones. On a previous occasion after heavy rain, a group from our Climbing Club was trapped at the hut for 24 hours because the river was impassable. When we arrived this time and had settled in, Jim went round to get water. He came back a few minutes later to pick up a cup to use as a ladle.

"The water runs very shallow over the slabs," he said followed by the immortal comment, "It takes a mug to get the water."

Rùm Direct

We were going to Rùm for a long weekend achieved after many failed attempts to get permission to go to the island. We kept getting letters saying that Rùm was full on our chosen weekend which rather puzzled us until we learnt that the authorities imposed a limit on numbers of visitors at any one time.

The ferry was due to leave at 06.00 so we slept in cars at Mallaig on the Friday night. Actually, one group slept in very comfortable but definitely illegal first class beds at the station (and I don't mean the police station). We went down to the pier at about 05.15 in a howling great gale to be told that there was no chance of sailing before mid-morning. We pottered around Mallaig and then the word was passed around that we would sail at 11.30, going via Armadale in Skye to drop off some passengers because their ferry would not be sailing.

We got onto the Lochmor with our sacks and proceeded out into the Sound of Sleat. The wind was not too bad and we wondered what all the fuss was about. We dropped passengers at Armadale and sailed down the coast of Skye and rounded the Point of Sleat. The Captain had already told us that if conditions became unfavourable he would turn back. When we rounded the Point, our world changed. To mainly landlubbers, the seas seemed to be impossibly high. We prayed that the Captain would not attempt to turn as the mountainous seas were away above us when we were in the troughs and we reckoned that we would be in danger of turning turtle if we turned broadside. Anyone staying below decks was being violently sick and it was not much better in the open. One of our group is never a good traveller and he was constantly being sick. It seemed to be non-stop for four or five hours and he could well claim the Guinness record boak! In fact, when we eventually got to land, he had to have his tent put up for him and he retired to it for the entire weekend.

If you have ever sailed on the Lochmor, you will know that it is a boat of just over 100 feet with three decks, one down near the water at the stern, one higher amidships above the cabin and one forward higher still above the bridge. The Captain told us that the waves were probably about 25 feet but they looked like Munros to us. The lower deck was unusable being constantly underwater. The result was that everyone was hanging onto a rail on the upper two decks or the gangway between them. With the violent pitching and yawing, the view veered from walls of water when in the troughs to water either a long way below you or very close at hand when on the crest depending on which side the boat was rocking to at the moment. What was rather off-putting was that, in addition to all of this, the boat climbed up each wave on full throttle and then throttled right back to slide down and go crashing with a thump into the trough where full power was applied again. At one point, I was hanging onto the railing on the gangway to the top deck beside Kate who looked rather ill and said that she was going to be sick. I offered to try to get her to the deck-rail but she said that she preferred to be sick where she was. She lived up to this comment but, in the circumstances, no-one was the least put out.

We were due to go to Rùm via Canna and were not fancying this one bit because, as we approached it, we would lose any slight protection that Rùm was presently giving us. We had already been told not to worry about the transfer to the flit-boats in Loch Scresort as, being east facing, it would be very calm. However, before that we had Canna to contend with.

Suddenly the bows started swinging to port and we realised that we were no longer going north of Rùm to Canna but, as hinted earlier by the Captain, were now going straight for Rùm.

Donald's voice sounded out from the forward deck. "Three cheers for the Captain."

A Rùm Do

We were making a return trip to Rùm one week after my sixtieth birthday so I arranged to take over a 72-pint barrel of Fraoch ale. I phoned McBraynes to find what it would cost to take it over and they gave me a price for the journey over and then back with the empty cask.

When we got to Mallaig, some of our party went to board the apparently only ferryboat in the harbour and we called them back. "That's not our boat. If you look under its stern you will see the Lochmor!" On the quay above our boat a tarpaulin with loops on the corners had been laid out. We had to pile our sacks on this and then it would be hauled onto the Lochmor by its stern-crane. I decided that there was no need to pay extra for my beer and added the barrel to the pile.

This all happened before the new deep water pier was built on Loch Scresort and the water was too shallow for the Lochmor to reach the old pier. It was necessary for us to transfer to a flit-boat for the transfer to shore. The crane started to lift the tarpaulin with its luggage but perched right on top was my barrel and it looked as though it might roll into the sea. Two of us ran forward to rescue it and were carrying it to the edge of the ferry to lower it to the flit-boat when the Captain opened a window on the end of the bridge. I thought that I was about to be presented with my carriage bill.

"Caledonian McBrayne has introduced a new rule today," said the Captain with a grin on his face. "You can bring as much drink as you want onto the Lochmor but you cannot take any off."

After walking the Rùm Cuillin ridge that day including what my mates informed me was an interesting view of me scaling the Askival Pinnacle in the kilt, we had a great ceilidh. We had more guests than expected. My barrel had been spied being unloaded and some of the residents came along to check its quality – "just to be sure, you understand." The day was a truly memorable late birthday celebration.

A Lucky Stroke

My wife Eleanor and I have an agreement that, except on longer trips, I do not phone home. Some remote locations are miles from public phone boxes and mobiles are inoperative. This arrangement avoids the worry of the non-arrival of an expected call.

On one occasion out in the islands, partway through the evening, I remembered that I had promised to make a call because it was Eleanor's birthday. By this time, the drink was flowing well and I called her on a mobile from the corner of the room. I apparently slurred my words and Eleanor jokingly asked if I'd had a stroke. I laughed it off and mentioned it to the others. All Eleanor heard as they formed a conga and moved around the room was them singing "Logan's had a stroke, boys, Logan's had a stroke."

To this day, if I ever slur one word, the refrain starts again.

Sailing Homeward

A party of Marilyn seekers had hired a small boat to take us to the small islands south of Barra in the Outer Hebrides. One of the group was Bert who is a great singer and I had a word with him before we sailed. I had an idea and he readily agreed to play his part.

After we had visited Sandray and Pabbay, our next stop was Mingulay. As we sailed towards the beach I opened my sporran and brought out song sheets for the Mingulay Boat Song and Bert led the singing.

The skipper could only look on in disbelief.

No Parking in Park

The area of Park on the east side of Loch Seaforth in Lewis is pretty remote unless you can get a boat in. I was in Lewis for a planned ten days to climb Marilyns. I had not brought a tent so it was impractical to camp out and climb the five hills which I wished to do in Park in one trip. Accordingly, I planned two separate long trips from the road-end at Eishken.

On the first trip, I did the three westerly hills in a horseshoe but was aware that I had left the two even more remote hills to the south and south-east. It was a tiring day that took eight and a half hours instead of the estimated seven. When I got back to the car, I bumped into a retired keeper who said that I looked knackered. I agreed with him that that was how I felt.

My holiday in the Outer Isles was nearing an end and I had climbed all the others hills which I had wanted to do. The weather had been unsettled and not the best to venture again into the wilds of Park. With not much time left, I wakened one morning in the hostel to good settled weather so returned to Eishken. The trip to the hills did not look too long at first glance on a map but, to start with, one had to walk west for over two miles to get round an extensive sea-loch before heading east to the hills. The first five miles or so got you only one mile south of the start and this had to be repeated on the return journey. For most of the day, I could hear gun-fire and could see small boats on the sea-loch. At the end of a day with lots of ups and downs and plagued by clegs, I eventually got back to Eishken. As I was staggering back to the car, I bumped into the retired keeper again and he insisted that I come to his house for tea and scones. While I was chatting to him and his wife, there was a knock on the door and the present keeper came in. He heard where I had been and I thought that he might be a bit annoyed that I had disturbed the stags. Not a bit of it. He just remarked that, if I had contacted him, he could have given me a boat-trip both ways over the sea-loch. A very kind offer but, in the circumstances, that is what I call a useless bit of information!

The Bressay Run

A group of Marilyn hunters had spent several days moving around the Shetland Islands ticking off their various hills. Next day we would be sailing to the Orkneys. One of the group had not climbed Ward of Bressay on the island just off Lerwick and time was running out. Jim, who had his camper-van with him, offered to take him there. Now, the hill has a service track all the way to the aerial at the top and, as time was short, when we came off the ferry, Jim offered to drive to the top – a slightly dishonest way of 'climbing' a hill. We all sat in the van whilst Jim drove up and, at the summit, someone remarked that we might catch the ferry before it left Bressay if we hurried.

Jim then drove us back down at some speed, especially for a camper-van, with loose chippings rattling on the chassis. As we drove onto the pier the ferry gang-plank was half up. The crew saw us coming and lowered it again and we got on.

I doubt if anyone has beaten that time for the round trip from Lerwick to Ward of Bressay and back.

Yell for a Ferry

I was back in the Shetlands again to climb Humps. I had a careful plan to climb the 14 hills in six days which is hard enough for me at my age. The plan almost went disastrously wrong on the first day. Jim and I came off the overnight ferry from Aberdeen and drove straight up Mainland Shetland to go over on two ferries to climb hills on Yell and Unst. Unknown to us, it was the day of the Yell annual show and ferries had been fully booked in advance. However, it appeared to be that a few spaces were left for possible emergency vehicles. We got onto the two ferries over and two back in these few spare places.

We did manage to get the 14 hills done comfortably with a day to spare. One unusual feature, which I had never heard of, was a Curry Stool Trig on the top of one of the Unst hills. If you don't know what that is, it is worth a trip to Shetland to see it at the same time as climbing some of the other hills.

Chapter 2 Furth of Scotland

2.1 England

The three-thousand footers as well as many other hills, in England. as well as those in Wales and Ireland, are well worth visiting, especially when stalking might curtail possibilities in Scotland There is just not the same feeling of isolation in any of the high hills furth of Scotland.

Lost on The Old Man

I had first met Peter from Yorkshire a good few years before in the Tomdoun Hotel near Loch Quoich. We had since met at least once a year, mainly in the Lake District. To celebrate the new millennium he was planning a trip round the 131 Wainwrights which were over 2,000ft. The Wainwrights are 214 hills in the Lake District described in Alfred Wainwright's seven volume Pictorial Guide to the Lakeland Fells. I had not long retired and offered to accompany him when I was available. He was still working but had taken sufficient time off work to get the trip done in one spell in early spring. He had booked space in various Fell and Rock Club huts so there was no need to carry camping kit around.

The trip began in mid-April but unusually late snow slowed progress and Peter had to delay the completion and go back to his work as a school teacher. There were only a few hills still to climb. The project was completed in a second spell in early June. In the event, I was available for both spells so I did the whole trip with him. It finished with a grand celebration on the summit of Scafell Pike followed by a massive party at Brackenclose near Wasdale Head.

One day, we did a section from near Wrynose Pass over Swirl How and Brim Fell to Coniston Old Man. It was very misty but crowds were milling around the large summit cairn. We then continued over Dow Crag and down west to hit the road near Seathwaite (not the one near Scafell Pike) where we had left a second car. We would drive from there round to Hardknott Pass and climb Harter Fell. As we approached the road near Seathwaite, we made up on a family of parents, son and daughter.

"Are we nearly at Coniston?" the father asked.

"The Old Man is the way you've just come," we said.

"I know," he said, "We've been up it and are going down to the town of Coniston."

"You've come off the wrong side of the fell," we said. "Did you not check your compass?"

They had no map or compass but had just taken the path from Coniston and, on leaving the top of the hill, had chosen the wrong one for descent. We directed them to Seathwaite to look for a bus or taxi.

A Wet Finish

Peter had assembled a lot of his friends to accompany me on my last Wainwright – Haystacks. The weather was diabolical with non-stop heavy rain but, as the others had come over from Yorkshire, we felt that we should push on. All was straightforward from Gatesgarth via Scarth Gap to the summit other than some greasy rock high up. To descend, we planned to continue to the old mine-workings where we could stop at a good shelter for lunch before descending by a path to Warnscale Bottom. However, just short of the shelter we met a problem – there was a raging torrent in between. I was near the back of the group and they had stopped at the water's edge.

Crossing the torrent

I could see plenty of boulders and the torrent looked wide but not too deep. I had walking poles so, with barely a moment's thought stepped in and got across with legs soaked up to the knees. I was surprised to be passed halfway over by a collie which successfully made it. Some people decided to go further up-stream looking for an easier crossing and we had to wait in the shelter nearly half an hour for them. Peter caused some amusement by involuntarily sitting down when halfway over and, I'm sorry to say, he got no sympathy.

I'm not so familiar with the Lake District but know that areas like Knoydart must be treated with great respect, or even avoided, in wet weather. There is so much rock in such areas that rivers can rise very quickly and form impenetrable barriers.

Kilts Away

I went up early one morning from Grasmere to Helm Crag which is topped by a rocky outcrop called, amongst other names, The Howitzer. I had passed several people on the way up but the summit area was deserted. It was a very windy day and, as I scrambled up the small crag to the very top, the up-draught blew my kilt right up towards my shoulders. By the time that I topped out and had reversed the scramble, no one had appeared. This is probably just as well as I might have been reported for indecent exposure!

A Hard Day's Fight

On a camping trip to the Lakes, Bill and I decided to have a go at climbing England's four 3,000ft. hills in a day using bikes between them. It was a blisteringly hot and sweaty day so we knew that the trip would not be plain sailing. At 5am we drove from our camp-site near Keswick to Thirlmere from where we climbed Helvellyn and were back to the car in 1 hour 35. After that we cycled to Skiddaw and, after climbing it, were back to the bikes again in 1 hour 35. It was then a long cycle to Seathwaite where we left the bikes. After a quick coffee, we went up the Corridor Route to Scafell Pike and over by Lord's Rake to Scafell. We returned to Scafell Pike and took in its two tops before working cross-country via Esk Hause and High Raise to the car. This part of the trip from bikes to car took just over 7.5 hours. To finish, we drove round to pick up the bikes before driving back to Keswick for a well-earned pint (or two). We calculated that the whole trip of 13 hours 20 from the car involved 20 miles on bikes, 25.5 miles on the hills and a total ascent of 9,250 feet. It makes me feel tired just to read the log these days!

Last and Lost

Although I had climbed quite a few Wainwrights over the years, once I had accompanied Peter on his Millenium trip mentioned earlier, I had very few left to complete the list. I don't get down to the Lake District so often so it was not until November 2009 that I climbed my last one. I felt pleased that another hill list was under my belt.

I was slightly deflated when Peter said that I should do another 30 hills which the Fell and Rock Club had listed as deserving to be added to Wainwright's list. I had only done a handful of these so set about ticking them off. I was ready to tackle the last one, Hare Shaw, in early 2011.

For this last hill I was joined by Peter and many of his friends from Yorkshire. They knew these hills well so I was not worried by not having a map of this outlying area. However, before we started out, I looked at someone's map and took a bearing from our starting point to the hill because I had been told that the countryside was pretty featureless. I hung back at the start so that the others could be at the top before me to welcome me. From the car, I could not see which direction they had gone in. I started out and took my bearing but could only spot four people ahead of me although we were a party of ten. I made up on them and said that the others must be moving fast as I could not see them in front. They told me that the others had gone to the right towards a prominent little peak some distance away. Remarkably, none of the five of us had a map but we all agreed we were on the right bearing.

We got to the summit and had to wait over 30 minutes for the others to arrive. They sheepishly admitted to going to the wrong bump. So my last Wainwright outlier was attained with little help from my Lake District 'experts'.

Plenty of Sheep

I was in a spell of climbing Marilyns (hills with a minimum drop all round of 150m) in the Pennines. One that I wished to go up was on military property but the first bit on a private road was protected by a locked gate but could be cycled. However, entry was barred if a red flag was flying. I had heard firing earlier in the day but when I got to the start point on the main road no flag was flying. There was a cottage a short distance down the main road and I decided to go there and see if they thought it was safe to climb the hill.

A lady answered the door and said that she was the shepherd's wife. She would consult her list of closure days. She could not find it and could not contact her husband on her mobile. However, she said that a couple of miles up the track was another gate. If I got there and there were sheep beyond it, it was safe to go on as her husband always moved the sheep out of that area on firing days.

There were plenty of sheep beyond the second gate so I got my hill climbed successfully.

A New Mountain

I was visiting my daughter in London and took the opportunity to borrow her car for a few days to climb some Marilyns in the south of England. One of these was Cliffe Hill just outside Lewes near Brighton. The top of the hill is in the middle of a golf-course and I was advised to go early before it got too busy. Strangers on their course were rather frowned upon. At 9am I strode up between two fairways wearing the kilt and shortly reached the trig point beside a green. Two golfers were putting out.

"What are you doing here?" one asked in a friendly manner.

"Didn't you know that this is one of the mountains of southern England," I replied somewhat cheekily.

"Gosh," he said. "I must tell the secretary."

Bumping into the Army

I was climbing a hill on Dartmoor where no red flags were flying but I could hear constant firing. After climbing the hill, I got onto a track that would take me back towards my car. It was taking me towards the firing but, still, there were no red flags up any of the flagpoles. Eventually, I came upon trenches just off the road to my left. They were full of soldiers apparently defending it from attackers further to the left. It felt strange to be nonchalantly walking past in the kilt nodding towards them. However, no one challenged me so I had not inadvertently drifted into a restricted area.

On another occasion, in the Kielder area in the north of England, I was climbing some hills in an area subject to army restrictions. Although I could hear distant firing, there were no flags on the poles at the entrance to the area so I drove in. After two or three miles, I came over a rise near the hill that I wanted to climb and saw army vehicles ahead. I could see soldiers firing from the road-side but away from my direction. I drove up and asked the officer in charge if I could climb my hill.

"Yes," he said, "because they are lousy shots but stay behind the ridge-line just in case."

2.2 Wales

The high hills compare well with those in Scotland and the weather is just as variable. However, I never felt the same feeling of remoteness. I did find, however, on the lower hills that some farmers and land-owners were very protective of their property and I sometimes had to find an alternative approach to a summit.

Adam and Eve

I had never been to Snowdonia before and we were camped at Williams' farm not far from Tryfan. A couple of us fancied scrambling up Tryfan's North Ridge, and carrying on up Bristly Ridge to traverse the Glyders before continuing to Elidir Fawr. Before we left camp, one of the others, Robert, reminded me that I would be expected to gain 'The Freedom of Tryfan' by stepping between Adam and Eve. I hadn't a clue what he was talking about so he had to explain that there were two natural obelisks on the summit, each above head height and slightly apart. I would have to surmount one and jump over to the other.

We scrambled up the North Ridge and eventually arrived at the summit to be confronted by Adam and Eve together with a large group of sun-bathers.

Tryfan from Williams' farm

Bill reminded me about the freedom but I was a bit hesitant, not because of the location, but because I was wearing the kilt in the proper manner. At any rate, I took the plunge, or to be more accurate, the slightly stretched stride between the rocks. I could not climb the obelisk closest to the cliff edge and had to go up the other one. This meant that my move was towards the cliff edge and I noticed that any slight overrun and you were straight over the cliff with a big drop to Heather Terrace.

We then carried on up Bristly Ridge to climb the Glyders. Partway up, we passed two Irish chaps who were struggling a bit. When I passed them in my kilt, one of them shouted to his companion that he could spot a good hold but he could not catch it as it was moving too fast. That got me moving even faster.

The rest of the day passed uneventfully and when we got back to camp, I remarked to Robert that the freedom leap was slightly dodgy because of the prospect if you overshot. "I wouldn't know," he said. "I've never done it."

Brecon Meeting

I had been to a business meeting in North Wales. It was over by lunch-time and I was not scheduled to have another meeting till next morning in Port Talbot in South Wales. It was a beautiful summer's day in the middle of a very dry spell and I decided to drive down through mid-Wales instead of travelling east to the M5/M50. As usual on these 'foreign' trips I was wearing the kilt to remind the natives that there is a proud nation north of the border.

As I approached Brecon in mid-afternoon, I suddenly had the idea that there was plenty of time to take in some of the Brecon Beacons. I stopped in the town and bought a brochure which described the route up over Y-Gyrn to Corn Du and Pen-y-Fan from the Storey Arms. When I got there, I was disappointed to find that, despite its name, the Storey Arms seemed to be an Outdoor Centre but was certainly not a pub. After the walk in the heat I fully expected to be looking for some liquid refreshment.

As the whole trip was unplanned I didn't have my hill clothes with me so had to go up in kilt and shirt and carrying a sweater. Luckily, I nearly always have a pair of boots lying around the car so I was well enough prepared for a walk on a cloudless day. There was no problem going up the tourist motorway and as I approached the main summit, kilt blowing in the breeze, I could see someone at the cairn. When I reached him, he greeted me in an Aberdonian accent with "Christ, I came here to get away from the likes of you." He did at least direct me to a lovely little pub further done the valley.

Three Peaks Encounter

This trip covered Wales, England and Scotland but, as it started in Wales, I have included it in the Welsh section.

We had started on the Three Peaks trip from Caernarvon at 8.30pm so that we could climb Snowdon before it got dark and then drive to the Lake District in the short night hours. All had gone to plan. We had topped out on Snowdon at about 10.15 and had plenty of light all the way back to the car which we reached at 11.20. We had then shared the driving to the Lakes and started up Scafell Pike just before 4.30am topping out at a quarter to six as a beautiful morning developed.

We had not been descending for long when we met a chap toiling up. He informed us that he had started out early to get the mountain to himself and we had quite spoilt his day. When we pointed out that we were doing the Three Peaks jaunt and described it to him, his only comment was that he wished that we had restricted it to Two Peaks and kept Scafell Pike out of it.

I know that he was no typical Englishman but no wonder that some Scots can develop an anti-English attitude when people like him are around.

Our route on Scafell Pike had been from Wasdale Head to Seathwaite which we reached at 7.20. Our driver had driven the long way round to meet us. He unfortunately had a bit of a hangover and when we reached Seathwaite he had only been there for half an hour and was suffering. I had to drive all the way to our Ben Nevis start at the top end of the Glen Nevis road. I was like a zombie climbing to The Ben by the Waterslide. The Ben took from 1.05pm to 4.02, having topped out at 2.40.

We successfully completed the Three Peaks challenge at the side of Loch Linnhe at 4.08pm. We had been determined to do it from sea level to sea level so were very pleased to have beaten twenty hours but we had been very fortunate with the weather all the way. I would, however, advise anyone doing the Three Peaks to include a non-climbing driver who can also prepare a brew-up for the others as they come off each hill.

I repeated the trip with my family thirty-one years later as a charity event to celebrate my forthcoming seventy-fifth birthday and it was a lot harder! However, that trip gave me my first clear day on Snowdon after several visits. This was the only 3,000-foot hill in the British Isles that I had not had a view from. In addition I learnt the marvels of modern electronics. On the summit, one of my daughters sent her friends a photograph and message saying the first peak had been climbed. The congratulations started to come through in a couple of minutes.

2.3 Ireland

Ireland is the Green Isle because it can rain quite a bit. However, in good weather it has many glorious remote hill settings – especially those close to the west coast.

Irish Crossing

Bill, Jim and I were making a quick dash over to Ireland to take in the Irish 3,000-footers. With the days available, we were going to be hard-pressed to climb them all. We travelled overnight from Holyhead, buying our duty-free on the boat. We reached Dublin in the early morning and went straight to the Wicklows to climb Lugnaquillia. We had checked that it was safe to do so because there is an army firing range on the slopes of the hill. This was during the Troubles and we got the cheery reply. "Absolutely safe. All the troops are up at the border." We then travelled cross-country to the Galtees. There was still enough time to climb Galtymore and drive on to Killarney thereby leaving us more time in coming days for Macgillycuddy's Reeks and Brandon.

I was reminded of an earlier visit when two carloads of us had travelled to Ireland and climbed Lugnaquillia on the first day. It was a more leisurely trip than the present one and we had booked ahead into the hostel near Galtymore.

Brandon Mountain – Final British Isles 3,000ft. hill for Bill and me.

The road-signs between the Wicklows and the Galtees were a nightmare and the cars got separated and totally lost somewhere close to the hostel. Instructions from locals seemed to be sending us in circles. As we approached one unmarked cross-roads intending to go straight over, our mates' car shot over in front of us on the other road. It was like the Keystone Cops.

On the present occasion, as we climbed Galtymore, we could see bad weather coming in from the west. It's an easy hill to climb with the so-called Black Road going well up. To avoid a wetting, Bill and I accelerated up the hill but Jim said that he would take his time. The black clouds were getting nearer as we breasted the hill and we ran most of the way back, passing Jim who was still plodding up.

Back at the car, the rain started and we knew that we had quite a wait in prospect so we opened a large bottle of duty-free Martini. I've never really liked that drink but it seemed to be okay that day. Anyway, by the time that Jim arrived back, we had almost emptied the bottle and were not exactly in a fit state to drive.

Shortly after continuing our journey, we stopped for petrol and I got out to stretch my legs. We had only just got going again when I realised that I had mislaid my drink. We returned to the filling-station to see the glass sitting atop a pump. I got some strange glances from other customers as we stopped, I shot out and grabbed my glass, and we drove off again.

Jim had to drive the whole leg to Killarney but our strategy allowed us to get all the hills completed.

Road Block

My family was accompanying me to Ireland on one of my jaunts to climb the three-thousanders. We sailed from Liverpool to Dublin and spent the first day sightseeing around the city.

We found it hard to find a place to park in the middle of Dublin. We were just about to leave the car in a side street with a lot of our gear on a roof-rack when we were approached by a local. "Don't park there," he said. "Your kit is liable to be removed from the roof. Park on a main road. Although that is not allowed, the Garda will see that it is a British car and leave it alone."

As usual, I was wearing the kilt and at one point, I stopped on a traffic-island in O'Connell Street to take a photograph along its length. Whilst lining up the shot, one of my daughters said "Dad, you'll have to stop. You're holding up the traffic."

Continuing to look through the viewfinder, I said "I'm no problem when

I'm standing on this traffic-island."

"Dad," she said, "stop taking photographs and look." I stopped and looked around. Standing in the middle of O'Connell Street was a large group of Japanese tourists holding up the traffic whilst they photographed me.

Playing Safe in Ireland

We had been on a week's walking in the hills up the west coast of Ireland and were crossing the border near Derry on our way home to Scotland. We had some hours in hand and decided to have a look around the city. The Troubles were at their height and we entered the somewhat intimidating compound at the border crossing to be confronted by an armed border guard.

After we had sorted out the problem that my passenger, Bill, had spent much of his life in Yorkshire and the soldier was a Lancastrian, I wondered aloud whether it would be wise to enter Derry wearing, as I was, a kilt. The soldier looked at me, thought for a moment, and then said "You will be all right. Firstly, the military does not wear the kilt in Northern Ireland. Secondly, unlike you, the military is not permitted to wear beards and, thirdly, you have played absolutely safe by wearing that Guinness T-shirt."

We got home that night and, in the late-night news, heard that someone had been shot in Derry that very day.

Band Aid

After a week's walking in the Irish hills, we were travelling across Ulster to get the ferry back to Scotland. We had time in hand so stopped off in Coleraine for a couple of hours. It was a gala day and the pedestrian precinct was teeming with people. We heard a brass-band in the distance and eventually tracked it down to a pub. They were in there for a short break (or so they told us) and were having a jam session. We got them to play a couple of Scottish favourites before they decided that it was time to resume their marching and playing around the pedestrian precinct. When they got up to go, it was obvious that one of their number was incapable of getting to his feet let alone playing. In fact, while we watched, he literally slipped under the table and fell asleep.

The band asked us if one of us would stand in for half an hour and play the chap's cymbals. We pointed out that we had only sat down to our pints but an arrangement was made. The two of us in our kilts marched along at the rear of the band. We each wielded a cymbal in one hand and drank from our pints in the other.

The Irish are something else!

Chapter 3 Europe

3.1 Around the Alps

The one thing which I have never got used to in the Alps is the sheer scale of things. A hill which seems to be only a short distance ahead and not too high can take an age to climb. Also, I never did enjoy the Alpine starts to climb the big hills. This is where you start in the middle of the night to be safely off the climb before the sun softens the snow making progress much harder. More importantly, it releases rocks from their icy grip and they come tumbling down the mountain sides.

I should make clear that, beyond the British Isles, Scottish hill-goers generally refer to every peak as a hill and not as a mountain. This includes Everest!

The Chamonix Committee

Our Club had organised a summer trip to Chamonix. Because it would coincide with Bill's sixtieth birthday, we decided to do things in style and organised accommodation in four flats in a block of the same. The organisation of the flats was such that, to get from two of the flats to the other two, you had to descend in a lift to the ground floor, cross a large entrance hall and ascend another lift at the far side.

Many of the flat occupiers were still in residence and a gentleman, who turned out to be the chairman of their organising committee, had occasion to speak to us. He reminded us that we were in their flats and could we please be a bit quieter and not keep rushing around the place.

One day, after a long overnight trip in the high Alps, we got back to the flats in early afternoon. After a shower, I decided to go over to see our colleagues in the faraway flats to share some refreshment. It was extremely hot, so I descended the lift in bare feet and wearing only shorts and carrying a bottle of wine. The doors opened on the ground floor and I stepped out to be confronted by a table round which the chairman and his organising committee were sat. It was too late to turn back so I strode over the hall wishing them 'Bonjour' and shot into the lift on the other side. You could have heard a pin drop, but we never had another visit from the chairman. I think he probably thought that we were beyond redemption.

Zermatt Adventures

We were camped at Täsch, the last place before Zermatt where the general public is allowed to drive to. We wanted to start with a relatively easy acclimatisation day so took the lift to the summit of the Klein Matterhorn, roped up and climbed the Breithorn. We carried on over to climb Pollux, which was not in our original plan and the second rope of three was struggling, so any thought of carrying on to Castor was forgotten about. The last moves to the top of Pollux were on very icy ground and we advised some Italians who were about to descend that they should keep out in the sun where it was not so icy. Whether they did not understand us, or chose to ignore us, the pair of them roped together proceeded to descend on the icy slopes in the shade. Within moments they were away and went sliding down the fortunately rock-free slopes with cries of "Gelido, Mamma mia!" We never heard of any disasters so presumed that they survived.

We started to descend north and soon became separated from our second rope of three who said that they were okay but would take their time. We came to a very steep convex slope of soft snow which looked as though it might avalanche. We therefore roped down it one at a time to a reasonably secure halfway stance and then repeated the manoeuvre to the bottom. Donald knew that an apparently easier route led to an area of séracs and had to be avoided. The second rope got benighted in this area as they found the séracs in the darkness – they realised that they would have to re-ascend to avoid them so had a very uncomfortable night on the slopes. We had an interminable journey down to and across the Gornergletscher and up to the top terminus of the Gornergrat railway. We were now in darkness and the last train had long since left. We walked down the railway-track to Zermatt. At one point, there was a hollow sound under our footsteps and Donald explained that we were going over a bridge and to keep away from the side. Next morning, when I saw the bridge from Zermatt, I was horrified. It is an enormous span over a gorge. We got down to Zermatt after all the pubs had closed and Donald and I lay down and fell asleep on the pavement whilst Ian went back to camp for his car. At one in the morning, you don't see police stopping you from driving up to Zermatt.

Next day, we went up to Zermatt to wait for the others to return. We found that a supermarket was having a promotion of a new wine and customers were being offered a sample glass. You then had the back of your hand stamped so that you didn't get another free glass. Every time I passed that corner of the store, I was given another glass although no one else got more than one. Eventually, the girl said that she liked the look of the kilt and was encouraging me to come back for more (if you see what I mean!). I kept Ian and Donald supplied with free wine. When the others eventually appeared off the train, they were rather displeased that our interest in the wine was greater than that of their well-being.

A few days later, we set off to climb the Monte Rosa. We took the Gornergrat railway and then walked over the Gornergletscher to the Monte Rosa hut for the night. When we got there Donald, who had stayed in the hut some years before, shot off to the toilets. When he came back, he said that the state of the toilets was disgraceful and the smell was terrible. A stranger who overheard this comment pointed out to Donald that these toilets had been closed two years before and the new ones were at the other end of the building.

Very early next day, we climbed with head-torches up to the Silbersattel between the Dufourspitze, the main summit, and the outlying Nordend. There was a very strong wind at the saddle and the steep slope to the main summit did not seem to be a sensible proposition in these conditions. Instead, we went out along to Nordend keeping back from the south-facing cornice and found that we were protected from the wind. The last climb to the summit of Nordend is a short scramble. Now as we traversed along to it, we had never seen over to the Italian side as we were down the slope slightly on the Swiss side. Donald led up to the summit and the route spiralled round towards the Italian side. He quickly reached the summit and called me to follow. He was taking in the rope and I was entering the last short chimney to join him. He asked me to pause a moment and look down. The fields of Italy were thousands of feet below me and I was at the top of what is one of the highest cliffs in Europe.

"You won't get a view like that in Scotland," was Donald's comment.

Courmayeur Capers

Our annual Alps trip was to be based in Courmayeur in the Aosta Valley in north-west Italy. The day before, Italy had beaten France in a World Cup qualifier. When we crossed into Italy on the Great St. Bernard Pass, the score was emblazoned all over the Customs building, the officials were well into their wine and we were waved through non-stop. This was in the pre-Common Market days when border crossing delays were often extensive for foreigners.

I had never been to Italy and did not appreciate the value of the lira. We stopped to pick up provisions in Courmayeur and I led the way into a public toilet in the square. The concierge asked me for 100 lira and I walked straight out and relieved myself in some waste ground off the street. Donald came out of the toilet laughing. "The cost was thrupence-halfpenny," he said. I was soon to find that any loose change due in a shop was given in the form of a handful of sweets.

Courmayeur

We set up camp in the official site some distance from the town and went to the local shop to buy wine supplies. We decided that one 1.5 litre bottle per couple every second day should suffice. Over the next few days, after we discovered how cheap the wine was, the consumption progressed through 1.5 litres per couple every day to 1.5 litres per person per day before stabilising at 2 litres per person per day. This, I should hasten to add, was only on rest days.

One of our major trips was an attempt on the Grandes Jorasses. We started off directly from our camp as opposed to the normal point nearer Courmayeur and so missed a vital notice. When we reached our planned stop for the night at the Boccalatte hut, we found that it was closed for renovations. Luckily, we had bivvy bags and food but were short of a night-cap. The front door of the hut was all boarded up with a gap at the bottom, but we could see about nine feet inside a bottle of wine. I ashamedly have to admit that, using a plank of building material lying outside, we managed to rescue the bottle. We had no water but were right at the snow-line, so set to melting snow for tea and cooking. Donald had brought with him a brand-new lightweight stove which he had tested at home. At this altitude, it just would not melt the snow the flame stayed stubbornly yellow instead of going blue. Its gas-bottle was separate and joined to it by a flexible tube. In shear frustration, he grabbed it by the gas-bottle, swung it around his head and with an oath, released it over the glacier below. As it arched over in the night-sky, its flame turned blue. "It's working now," said Gordon.

Next day, we got up to Pointe Whymper and started the traverse to Pointe Walker. By this time, it was getting late in the morning and the snow was getting soft and heavy. We abandoned the traverse when we saw through a hole in the cornice to the fields of France. A pretty horrific descent on mixed ground led to a second night on the mountain. At one point, when I was second on a rope, we descended a knife-edge arête with incredibly steep icy slopes on either side. I shall remember till my dying day being told that, if my lead was to fall off one side, I had to jump off the other.

We only had one regret about this trip. The Club members who had stayed in camp told us that we had missed the very pleasant sight of a nearby group of German Fräuleins who had spent the day sunbathing dressed only in shorts.

One morning back at camp, we wakened up after an especially cold night. Donald wandered down to the toilet-block. The toilets were in cubicles but each was simply a hole in the ground with a constant run of water coming along a gutter at roof level with an offshoot into each latrine. Donald came running back. "Quick, go and use the toilets now. The water has frozen in the night and they will soon be unusable." We quickly used them but he was right. Half an hour later a gas-mask would have been necessary.

On our last evening, we went out for a meal and, with our group of 12, the eating-house was obviously going to do quite well. As a thank-you, the proprietor provided free home-made grappa which everyone found quite revolting. We were seated in an alcove with a shelf behind us lined with potted plants. I'm afraid that when the proprietor was looking the other way, his plants got a liberal dosing of grappa.

We had been going to the same taverna each night and after our final meal, we returned there for the last time. I wanted to celebrate with a cigar and eventually got through to the barman what I wanted. He disappeared through a bead curtain into the back-shop and returned with an enormous cigar in a metal container. He would not take any money for it. As I was contentedly puffing away in a corner, an old wizened face peeped through the curtain and then retreated. Immediately, there was the sound of very raised voices from the other side. Donald turned to me. "They've given you his cigar, you know."

I acted as the bank for all expenditure and paid the camp bill at the end of the trip. It was actually quite cheap but sounded ridiculous at three quarters of a million lira. When I redistributed the small change from the kitty, Donald chucked his in the bushes with a comment (to the effect) that it was useless.

Wine at the Goûter

We were on our way home from Courmayeur via the Mont Blanc tunnel and decided that there was time in hand to climb the hill if we went to the Goûter Hut that day. After three weeks in the Alps, funds were running low so we knew that we could not afford the food and drink that would be on offer at the hut.

We went up from Les Houches by way of the téléphérique and tramway and eventually reached the rocky spur leading up to the Goûter. I was wearing the kilt, intending to leave it at the hut when we made our attempt on the summit the next morning.

We were halfway up the spur when a violent hailstorm suddenly descended on us and the temperature plummeted, and visibility went. The others stopped to pull over-trousers over their shorts but that posed a problem with the kilt. I therefore decided to scramble on up. After about ten minutes, the hail stopped and visibility improved such that I saw the hut just above me. People were coming back out onto the terrace and saw me in a kilt emerging out of a snowstorm. By the time that I had reached the terrace quite a crowd was watching me, and one chap stepped forward and thrust a half-bottle of wine and a glass into my hands, pointed at the kilt and gave a thumbs up. I shall never forget the looks on my mates' faces when they arrived and saw me sitting on my rucksack sipping a glass of wine.

Early next morning, we failed on the attempt on Mont Blanc because we got surrounded by a violent thunder and lightning storm. We could not even get into the Vallot Hut to shelter because the lightning was constantly striking its roof. Some years later, we got turned back at the same point by gale-force winds. A Scottish climber was blown to his death off the Bosses Ridge that morning.

Fear

Some years ago, I walked the Grande Randonnée 5 (GR5) from Lake Geneva to Nice. The first few days went well but the weather began to threaten as I left Samoëns. I was planning to pass the Alfred Wills Refuge, go over the Col d'Anterne and stop for the night at the chalet-refuge beyond the top. Halfway to the Alfred Wills, the heavens opened, the wind blew up strongly and a thick mist came down. Ominously, I could hear thunder in the distance but, of course, could see nothing.

The thunder came closer and closer and eventually, the mist was being lit up by the lightning flashes. It got to the point where there was no delay between the flashes and the thunder. I could not see if there was any shelter, so I began running blindly in the direction of the refuge. By now water was streaming off the hillside and the rain was so torrential that I was soaking and starting to shiver. I was never so glad to see the refuge emerge out of the mist. The warden persuaded me not to go any further, but I had no intention of doing so in these conditions.

Two days later I learned that a walker had been killed by lightning less than 10 kilometres away in the same storm.

National Celebrations

It was Bastille Day on the GR5 and we were close to Briançon. By now I had teamed up with my neighbours, Bill and Christine, who had started out on the walk shortly before me. We were climbing to the Col de Dormillouse and they stopped for a rest and a bite to eat. I said that I would wait for them at the col. I got there and the first people up after me were a group of about twenty French. I got out the camcorder and asked them to do something relevant to Bastille Day.

That is why I have a wonderful recording of a group of French people singing the *Marseillaise* on a col high in the Alps. I, of course, had to reply with *Flower of Scotland* which they all seemed to be aware of from rugby internationals. Bill and Christine arrived shortly afterwards and asked if they had been hallucinating!

Taxi for Logan

As we neared Nice, Bill and Christine took a different finishing route. My wife, Eleanor, and daughter Julie joined me for the last three days on the GR5. They had done very well on the first nine-hour day which ended with us in a rather poor self-catering gîte because the local hotel had closed. They had only agreed to join me because the accommodation towards the end of the walk was much superior if a trifle more expensive. We were lucky to get any food that evening because everything was shut but one shop opened for an hour in the evening.

Next day was very, very hot and, by the halfway point at Levens, we were all dead-beat. We still had about three hours walking to do. Julie made the comment that, if there was a bus from there to our stopping point at Aspremont, she would take it. To cut a long story short, Eleanor haggled with a taxi-driver and arranged a lift for the two of them. To make it easier for me, they took most of my luggage and left me with a small rucksack loaded with water. I estimated that I would reach Aspremont by 5pm. I would phone from the mobile if there were problems.

After a three-hour walk in extremely sweltering conditions I entered Aspremont at 4.55 and went straight into the Tourist Office to ask where our pre-booked hotel was. I was round there a couple of minutes after 5. We were lucky to get accommodation because, somehow, I had managed to book rooms in a hotel of the same name in northern France. The chap at the desk said that my wife and daughter had gone out for a walk so I had a quick wash and settled down with a beer. After half an hour, they had still not appeared, so I did a quick tour of the small town without success then went back to the hotel and had another beer. I don't know if it was the effect of the heat, but it never occurred to me to try to phone them.

Sometime after 6 they returned and I heard their incredulous voices as they were informed by the Manager that I was out in the beer-garden. They came out and their emotions veered between relief and anger. They had left the hotel just before 5 to meet me. We reckon that, at that moment, I must have been in the Tourist Office. They had then walked a considerable distance up the first hill crying out plaintively for me and then returned worried stiff thinking that they would have to report me missing. At least they had feelings for me.

Tunnels & Falls

We were staying in Grasse with my brother-in-law and his wife. I had a day to myself and decided to go for a walk in the hills. I would be dropped off in Gourdon, a hill-top village, and walk back down from there. I was duly dropped off and enquired of a local if there was a path down towards Grasse. He directed me to the end of the village and said that a walker's signpost would keep me right. I found the start of the route and then found that there was a choice of descent – one out in the open and the other, which I was told went periodically into tunnels, following the water-supply pipeline to Cannes. I chose the latter route as sounding a bit unusual. It did not have any route markers which should have warned me that it was not a normal route of descent. It was alright where tunnels were dead straight. However, where a tunnel had bends in it, it became pitch black and I had no torch with me. I had to carefully feel my way down these sections but luckily it had no steps in it. The views from occasional windows were truly magnificent. Eventually, I came out of the last tunnel just before a quarry but could not find the open-air path which was obviously meant to be the walkers' descent route. I went into the quarry offices to enquire. My French is awful and I could not get my question understood so they called in a worker who could speak English. He misunderstood me and thought that I was trying to climb from Grasse to Gourdon. "You go over the road and slightly downhill, you will see the route marker. Do not go into the tunnel where the pipe comes out. It is very dark in there and, even with a torch, people have panicked and turned back."

Some things you do not want to know beforehand.

A few days later we all went out with members of a French walking club into the hills on the Italian border. The day started in glorious weather but steadily deteriorated and it started to rain. The French all put on capes which totally enveloped them and their rucksacks. Kitted out in that gear, they all looked identical. We were traversing a hillside on a path when there was a cry at the front of the crocodile and a figure started to roll down the hillside. The fall was stopped by a tree a short distance down the slope. We found that it was one of the ladies in the party. She had been winded and was shaken but otherwise unhurt. I was a bit surprised that someone phoned the rescue service and said that a call-out might be required if she needed help later to get off the hill. I volunteered to carry her rucksack back to the car and we all got back safely. Returning home, in the outskirts of Nice, we were somewhat alarmed when a car wheel came flying down the road towards us. We swerved round it and, at the top of the hill, found that a car had shed a wheel without apparently being in an accident. We commented that things happen in threes, but we got back to Grasse with no further excitement.

No Black-out

I was with a group doing a refuge to refuge hike in the Austrian Tyrol. We wakened up one morning to a typical dreich Scottish day – overcast and very wet. The forecast was not good but one prediction was unusual and we were all looking forward to it. There was to be a 97% solar eclipse starting just before noon (Austrian time). We tramped along in the gloomy weather and the time of the eclipse came and went without any perceptible darkening of the sky. That really summed up what a terrible day it was.

3.2 Norway

My limited experience of Norway is of very poor paths and signage making navigation quite hard. Also, access to the open hillside was problematic in many places due to fenced compounds. However, my main memory is of the exorbitant price of beer.

Kilt at the Troll Wall

We were on holiday in Norway not far from the Troll Wall so it couldn't be missed. After gawping at the amazing climbing wall we drove round the back to where a main road goes over a pass at a considerable height. We went up the easy slopes to the top of the wall and looked down. It is an awesome sight made more so by the cracks along the top about fifteen to twenty feet back from the edge. Bits of the edge certainly look as though they are not destined to stay there forever or even much longer.

We returned to the car, which was in a car-park outside a restaurant and a chap ran up to me.

"Can I take your photograph," he said.

"Sure," I said "but why?"

"Well," he said, "I've just spent three months in Scotland and never seen a kilt and now I meet someone wearing one in Norway."

I know that we have some good hills in Scotland but the view behind me as he took the photo was going to take some beating.

Cheaper than the Skye Bridge

We were staying at a farmhouse near Åndalsnes in Norway and decided one day to drive up to Kristiansund to drive over the Atlantic Highway. With all of its fjords, the Norwegian roads have a large number of tunnels, bridges and long detours inland similar to the road round Loch Eriboll on the Scottish north coast.

The Atlantic Highway has been constructed to get away from the inhospitable coastal terrain on the mainland. We joined it at the east end and we hopped over a series of islands before rejoining the mainland further west. As with most of the bridge and tunnel links in Norway, there were tolls to be paid, although I now understand it to be toll-free. It turned out that the tollbooths were at the west end of the Highway and, as we had entered it from the east end, we would be paying as we left it. Our party, in two cars, had

The Atlantic Highway

stopped at one of the intermediate islands to take photographs and Bill and I, both wearing kilts, said that we would walk on. We eventually reached the tollbooths ahead of the others and, as we had left our money in the cars, sat down to wait on the crash-barrier opposite the toll-booth.

The attendant looked out.

"What are you waiting there for?" he said in immaculate English.

"Our friends following behind with our money," we replied.

"What do you want money for?" he said.

"To pay you the 160 kroners for two pedestrians."

"People in kilts go free."

"What about the two busloads just coming up in kilts?" we joked. He almost fell out of the booth window while looking out to see if this was true. It turned out that he had just returned to Norway after several years in Invergordon. When the cars arrived, we enjoyed watching the others paying the toll.

Postscript

Before we had gone on the trip to Norway, we discovered that the owner of the farmhouse where we were to be staying was originally from Yorkshire. She warned us of the price of beer in the country and offered to brew beer for us if we sent her some kits. We took her up on this and it saved us a small fortune although it ran out before the end of our holiday.

Chapter 4 Africa

4.1 Morocco

Out of courtesy to local customs, the kilt has not visited this country of lush lower slopes rising to a desert type terrain.

Photo Opportunity

I have spent some time out in Morocco with a Scottish guide who will be well-known to many of you. He likes climbing Munros but is not, you understand, a ticker! Understandably, he will not allow me to wear the kilt out there because one is not meant to display bare flesh.

On one occasion, we had climbed Oumzra (3,451m) and the weather broke as we got back to camp. The wind was threatening to cause us major problems so we retired to accommodation in a local village. We were pinned down in the village for 24 hours. I had one somewhat embarrassing experience when a young lad came up to me and said "Bonjour, monsieur. Ça va, là-bas." This is the normal welcome by people looking for something and is normally followed by the hand being proffered with a request for "Une dirham, monsieur." In this case, I got in first and said this. The young lad looked very shocked and retreated. I subsequently found that he was the headman's son and such a person would never beg.

In mid-morning, when the rain had stopped, I was asked to descend from the village to the riverside to see if the bridge which we needed to use for our escape had survived. It had but, by the time that I got back to report, our group had heard the news from a local and had packed and were ready to go. I was greeted with the words that I would soon make up and they went on their way. By this time, the sun had come out and it was back to scorching weather. I had got quite sweaty racing down to the valley and back and was a bit annoyed that I had been left behind. I rebelled and put on shorts and T-shirt, packed my sack and started out sometime after the others.

I descended to the riverside and made up on a Berber lady with her kids taking the washing down to the river. We had been told that, for religious reasons, many women do not like to be photographed. I signalled as to whether I could take a photograph of her and she was quite happy so I took the shot and moved on. Round the next corner I came upon one of our party, Gary, and asked him to hang on a minute. The lady came round the corner and I signalled that I would like a photograph of her and I together. She was quite happy so Gary duly obliged. We went on our way again and the lady took a branch path to the waterside whilst we kept higher up the hillside. We soon made up on the rest of the group and our leader was facing the river while I waved a final goodbye to the Berber lady and got a friendly wave in return.

"Who's she waving at?" asked our leader.

"Heaven knows," said I in all innocence.

This walkout had an amusing climax. We learnt that our planned exit down the valley was cut off because a bridge had been swept away. We would have to re-ascend to one of the highest main-road passes in the Atlas Mountains, the Tizi-n-Test, and try to get a lift down the road to our planned exit point where our Land Rovers would be waiting.

Four of us pulled ahead of the rest of the party but knew that up at the top of the pass was a shop where we could get sustenance. The Land Rover track up to the pass had been quite badly damaged by the storms and we met a lorry going down to start repairs. It was a long walk out and at the Tizi we waited and waited. Eventually, John spotted a lorry coming up the side track and got his binoculars onto it. "I do not believe what I am seeing," he said as he passed the binoculars to each of us. Not only was the rest of our party on the back of the open lorry but so were our three mules. The lorry took us down the main road to the nearest town with overnight accommodation from where we met our Land Rovers the next day.

Clearing the Board

Our travels around the Atlas Mountains were considerably eased by using mules to carry our heavy kit. They were under the control of Berber muleteers who also prepared our morning and evening meals which were taken in a communal mess tent. Facilities in this tent were pretty primitive with no seats unless you had the foresight to bring your own light folding one. You therefore sat around on rugs. It was pretty crowded and food plates had to be carefully balanced on the often sloping floor.

Charles had had a couple of unfortunate incidents where he had overturned the contents of his plate. However, on this occasion, the meal was safely behind us and we were reading books or chattering away. The muleteers had got a large piece of flat rock and had scratched a grid on it. Using dark and light coloured pebbles, they were playing a board-game.

Charles decided that the gas light was making the place quite hot so went to take off his jacket. As he swung it off, it swept over the board-game wiping all the pebbles to the floor. The game was apparently declared a draw.

The M'goun Gorge

One of the most magnificent treks that I have made was through the M'goun gorge. As you walk in towards the narrowest part, being forced to constantly cross and re-cross the river, the walls get steeper and steeper, higher and higher and closer and closer. At the really narrow part, you can touch both sides of the vertical cliffs rising hundreds of feet and there is no choice but to wade this stretch as all ground is under water. It is not a place to be in in time of flood and the area is known for its tragedies. When we went through in the dry season the water barely reached our knees.

The M'Goun Gorge

This stretch was one of the few places where the muleteers rode the beasts – they normally walk beside them – and their cries of encouragement echoed along the gorge. At one point, prone to serious flooding, there is an incredible path emerging out of the gorge constructed from a zigzag of rock ledges and wooden trestle platforms climbing up an inset corner. Some tremendous photographs and camcorder shots were taken and it is a trip never to be forgotten. One of the group had been quietly counting and in camp that evening told us that we had, in the course of the day, crossed the river 91 times and the previous day 26 times.

Searching for Mules

We had camped in the Atlas at a height of 2,500m. Next day, while the mules went round a long low-level route and up a valley, we were planning to climb 1,100m to Tinergwet. We would then have a sizeable descent and re-ascent to Awlim before retracing to the tizi or col between them to drop down to where we should find our camp. That, at any rate, was the theory.

As usual, under Hamish's control, we were off at the crack of dawn and we made good progress. As we got higher, we could see over towards Awlim. Our hearts sank. The whole northern side of the range was steep ice and snow and we had no ropes. We put on crampons and with axes got up Tinergwet. Views from the top confirmed our fears. It would be suicidal to go on. We would have to retrace and chase the mules.

After retracing our steps from Tinergwet we kept high to take in another unavoidable 3,000m peak and were now going to be putting the best part of two days into one. One of the party was not going well and we were clearly running out of time. I was shown on a totally inadequate map roughly where the camp should be and was sent ahead to find it and say that we were coming but from the opposite direction. My map was very poor, my Berber non-existent and my French very basic. I was not a very reliable messenger!

There were several paths to choose from and I often doubted whether I was going the right way. I was worried stiff, feeling that a lot was resting on my shoulders. Until I found the muleteers, they would not know where to look for us. Daylight was going. I could not even find the names of villages I was passing. As the last light was going, I came to a village and tried some basic French. A chap started muttering about "trois noir et trois blanc mulet." We had three black and three white mules so I guessed that he was talking about our group. He understood a thumbs-up sign and organised two guides with torches and we set off in the darkness high up on the side of a valley. They kept repeating "Une heure" which was rather dispiriting. I was so tired that I was going along on automatic when, suddenly, one of the guides saw lights in the bottom of the valley going in the opposite direction. He shot down the slope whilst the other guide waited with me. Ten minutes later, I was overjoyed when he returned with Ali, our chief muleteer, who had been out looking for us. I explained the situation to Ali, whose English is excellent, and suggested that the two guides return to the village and wait for the others to appear and bring them up to the camp. After I had consumed the whole contents of Ali's flask of mint tea, we continued to the camp where, thankfully, they had put our tents up. Ali had done well and got the camp far further up the valley than we had expected which, of course, made our journey from the wrong direction even longer. I got back to the camp at 8.15pm and the others were escorted in at 10.30. They would have been even later if they had not left in accommodation in the last village the member of the party who was feeling ill.

A Fortunate Encounter

We had camped high in the Atlas Mountains at a tizi (mountain pass) and next day four of us were going to traverse west along a rocky ridge to Jbel Tizel (3,066m). We were told that, once at the summit, we should continue west for some distance before descending south as much of the valley walls below the summit had been scoured out into cliffs. There were very few escape routes. Also, we knew that, after two weeks of blazing heat, rain was forecast for this area after three years of drought.

We got to our summit and continued west. Morocco maps leave a lot to be desired and it was not clear where we should descend south. We could see clouds coming towards us from the west so it looked as though the forecast was right. We saw one or two possible descent gullies but were reluctant to commit ourselves.

In the middle of nowhere, we spotted a nomad outside a cave. We ran down the hill to intercept him before he disappeared and said the name of the valley that we were trying to descend to. He motioned us to follow him. He took us over the next rise and pointed to a dip to the south and indicated to us that that was the way to go. We started off and, literally within five minutes, the weather hit us. We were enveloped in heavy rain and thick mist but had got a bearing just in time. We descended in virtual zero visibility occasionally being diverted by big drops beneath us. At one stage, a girl in the party had to disappear behind a rock and came out muttering "Oh to be a boy!"

After a long descent laterally on a steep, slabby hillside streaming with water, we thankfully got down to the road for the long walk back to our gîte.

It rained for most of the night. Next day as we passed in our Land Rover on the way back to Marrakesh we were aghast at what we saw. Our descent looked impossibly steep and was now plastered in snow.

Motorbikes on High

We traversed under Jbel Anzig (3,411m), which we had climbed the previous day. Today we were going up another big one – Imejdag (3,444m). We were in a very remote area, two days from the nearest Land Rover trail-head. The only people we were likely to meet here were Berber shepherds and nomads.

We had passed the tizi at the base of the final slopes and were following a rough mule-track which we knew traversed the peak a few hundred feet below the top. We would have to cut off it higher up to go for the summit. Suddenly, behind us, we heard a most unexpected noise – the internal combustion engine. This was impossible here. We looked around and saw a string of about seven or eight trail-bikes coming up behind us. They stopped some way back.

We carried on and left the track to go up to the summit. The bikers restarted and continued along the track beneath us. Just as we reached the summit, a group of men appeared from another direction. It turned out to be the bikers who had left their bikes below on the track to come up to the summit. We got talking to them. They were Frenchmen and they toured the Atlas in early spring and late autumn when they were less likely to annoy any others on the hill. For this reason, they had held back when they saw us ahead. They got lots of useful information from Hamish about trips they were planning for the next few days.

We continued on our way, passing their bikes which we looked at rather enviously, to drop into the valley. But we had almost bitten off more than we could chew. It was a very dry season with little water on the hills. The muleteers had been instructed to go down the valley to the first decent water supply. They had had to go for miles into what was planned to be part of our next day's route. We eventually found them just as darkness fell. Being at a good water-hole, we were surrounded by large numbers of sheep, goats, camels and some mules. The noise was incredible but I was so tired that, after dinner, I crept into my sack and was asleep in seconds. My tiredness might have been something to do with the fact that, unknown to me, our esteemed leader had slipped a small rock into my sack at lunch-time to slow me down.

Icy Toubkal

I had recently retired so decided to treat myself to two consecutive tours organised by Hamish. There was a week between them so Hamish got me accommodation with one of the locals in Imlil who provided mules for Hamish's tours. He also arranged for a guide to take me up to the Neltner Hut so that I could have a go at climbing Toubkal which is the highest peak in the Atlas Mountains.

The day before the attempt, I was led up to the hut by a guide. It was the very beginning of April and, well before the hut, we hit increasing amounts of snow and ice so I was glad that I had brought the ice-axe and crampons.

Next morning, I was up at 05.30 and away just after 6 with crampons on. I had been told that the hardest part of the trip was climbing out of the corrie that the hut was in. This was because it was an extensive boulder field. I need not have worried because everything was under very firm hard-packed snow – ideal for crampons. I strode up the middle of this snow-field but what surprised me was that very few of the others on the climb were wearing crampons and they were really struggling.

I went most of the way with two Germans but, when we reached the upper very icy slopes, I left them behind. The summit was almost deserted. After I returned to the hut, I had plenty of time in hand so descended back to Imlil. This saved another noisy night in the hut.

Marrakech Meeting

A group of us on one of Hamish's tours were sitting outside a café in Marrakech enjoying mint tea and cakes. We were chatting quite loudly because we were only feet away from noisy traffic. A stranger from a nearby table obviously heard us speaking in English and wandered over to us. He was from England and enquired as to what we were doing in Morocco. We explained that we were just about to start a walking tour in the Atlas Mountains.

He said that the best way to see Morocco was to go with Hamish Brown. He knew him very well and his tours were excellent. Hamish never said a word. After more chat, the stranger left.

"You never introduced him to us," said one of our group.

"I've never seen that man before," said Hamish.

Morocco Finale

At the end of five weeks in Morocco I had had my fill of couscous and tazines. Whilst waiting between planes at Heathrow, I dived straight into Harry Ramsden's for a large fish supper.

4.2 Tanzania

Another land of great contrasts from lush jungles to the highest point in Africa. Very friendly people who loved the kilt which has a passing resemblance, especially in its tartan, to their Masai clothing.

Training for Kilimanjaro

I fancied having a go at Kili before I got too old and thought that in 2003 at the age of 64 I'd better get a move on. I knew that technically it was no more than a plod – albeit a big one. I felt that my regular visits to the Scottish hills would keep me fit enough. The big question was how would I react to the altitude of nearly 6,000m. In the Alps, I had had no trouble at over 4,000m and I had been up to that height in Nepal in 2002 and to nearly 4,500m on Mount Whitney at the end of the John Muir Trail. I had seen how others suffered at these altitudes so was confident that, if I had any problems, they would occur above the top camp on Kili at 4,600m. To play as safe as possible, I chose a six-day trek up the hill with the third day being an acclimatisation one. On day three, the walk went across the southern face at between 3,800 and 4,600m but ended at 3,900 only 100m above the start of the day.

In the run-up to the trip in July 2003 I got out into the Scottish hills quite frequently. I had no idea who else might be on the trip. Although I move quite fast in the hills, I knew that Kili was more of a young person's game so I was concerned that I might be a hindrance. I need not have worried. Although three of the others were in their early thirties and the other two in their late forties, not too much training had been done. Clionadh had climbed Croagh Patrick in Ireland about a month before and Richard had recently done the Three Peaks (Snowdon, Scafell Pike and the Ben). The others appeared to have done little preparation. On the eve of the climb, Clionadh announced her main training effort. She was giving up smoking for the next six days.

The Approach

We were collected from our hotel in Moshi at 8.30am and it was bucketing – not really what I had expected in sunny Africa. We were driven to the Machami gate and, after the signing-in formalities, were on our way. The first day was a bit of a nightmare with non-stop rain and many diversions round waterlogged and deep mud sections on the track through the forest. Due to the conditions, what should have taken a leisurely six hours stretched to well over seven. I had brought a poncho which was a lifesaver because rain got into all of our luggage despite everything being in poly bags. The only dry thing was my day-sack under the poncho. If it carried on like this, we were not going to have the vital dry clothes for the cold summit bid. Thank heavens the first night's camp was already set up when we got there.

Next morning, Richard had his breakfast and promptly brought it up again. It rather put the rest of us off our food. His wife, Julia, felt sick and would probably have improved if she had been. Ian felt absolutely rotten. This was not a very auspicious start although the two Irish sisters and I were feeling fine. An hour up the trail, Ian was violently sick and then felt a lot better but later had a relapse. Day two, dry but in non-stop mist, took nearly 6.5 hours against the predicted 5 due to these problems. At least in the late afternoon at Shira camp, the mist drifted away and the sun came out with stupendous views of our mountain. We managed to get most of our clothes dried out.

Day 3 was the acclimatisation day. Richard lost his breakfast again and immediately felt great. Julia was still feeling sick and Ian felt a lot better. We were going to try to put one and a half days into one to make the last day before the summit bid a short one. We were in glorious weather with barely a breeze but below us the whole landscape was covered in cloud with only

On the way in to Kilimanjaro

Meru Peak poking through. This was to be the pattern until the final descent to the exit gate on day 6. We got to Barranco in early afternoon and, although Clionadh was now feeling sick, we decided to go on for several hours more to Karanga camp. The day's walk was over 11 hours and we had dinner after dark but we had left ourselves only a half day to reach the top camp at Barafu.

On day 4, Ian and Julia were still feeling ropy but we reached our top camp at 1130 and promptly dossed in our tents because we would be starting out for the summit at 11pm that evening. This early start is to ensure that the return from the summit to a camp well down the hill almost 3,000m below could be achieved in daylight. The summit day can take from 12 to 18 hours and it gets dark before 7pm. After an early dinner, we put on most of our clothes for the summit climb and tried to get some rest. I think that most people were too excited to sleep much. So far, I had worn the kilt the whole way but I was warned that it would be extremely cold on the summit so I dressed with trousers and long-johns under the kilt – maybe not traditional but I was thinking of my well-being!

The Summit Bid

After a cup of tea at 11pm, we were on our way under a full moon. Although most other parties – there must have been over 100 people in various groups – were using head-torches, we found that they were totally unnecessary. We did, however, have quite frequent stops for Ian and Julia. After two parties had passed us, our chief guide, Wilson, said that we were going too slowly and to guarantee success, at least for some, he would move ahead with a faster group whilst his two assistants ascended with the slower group. He was happy that Clionadh and I nominated ourselves for the fast group and we rapidly pulled ahead in the darkness. Clionadh's sister, Grainne, could have come with us but insisted on staying with Ian, her boyfriend – a case of true love winning over family and personal ambition.

After a seemingly endless trudge up the lava slopes, our group reached the volcano rim at dawn just after 5am. After all the illness that the party had suffered I kept waiting for my turn. It never came but I was pretty tired by this stage. We had another hour or so to traverse round the crater rim to the main summit, Uhuru. I had hoped to take my trousers off from under the kilt for the final approach but thought better of it when someone pointed out that the temperature was at least -15°C. We reached the summit at about 6.15 and after the obligatory photographs started back. We were actually so tired that we had no immediate sense of achievement that we had reached the highest point of Africa. That realisation only kicked in later.

Twenty minutes back from the top, we met the second party now containing only Ian, Grainne and one guide. Julia had found the effort to be too great so had descended from near Stella Point with her husband, Richard, and the other guide. With Richard, another case of true love....etc. We reckoned that this second party was probably an hour behind us. Ian looked dead beat but was determined to go on. We thus expected that we would have a two-hour lunch break back at our top camp instead of the planned one hour one before descending to Mweka for the night. As we descended, it turned into another beautiful day and I stripped into T-shirt and kilt at about 5,300m, definitely a case of the kilt on high. We got back to Barafu camp at 11am after exactly 12 hours and found Richard and Julia safely back. Wilson sent them with a guide to Mweka camp immediately as Julia was feeling very weak and he wanted to get her to a lower altitude. We would wait for the others to arrive in an hour or so, have lunch and then follow Richard and Julia down. That, at any rate was the expectation.

The Epic

In the hot sun I fell asleep in my tent, half wakening at times and thinking that we were being left undisturbed for a long time. Eventually, I came to in the middle of the afternoon and could hear urgent voices outside my tent. I got out to investigate. The guide who had been with Ian and Grainne had arrived back on his own to say that Ian's legs had given out and he was stuck on the hill unable to walk. He would need to be assisted if not carried down. He was still a good way up the hill out of sight hidden by lower slopes. Wilson sent up four porters and phoned Mountain Rescue to come up to our camp with a stretcher. Eventually, the porters arrived back with Grainne and Ian at 5.50. Ian had had to be half carried down for a considerable distance. It was now within an hour of darkness and the rescue party with a stretcher had not yet appeared from a lower camp.

Some porters were left at the top camp with Ian, who was warmly wrapped up in a tent, whilst Wilson, Clionadh, Grainne and I started down for a lower camp with most of the porters and luggage. It was now so near to darkness that we could not go right down to the camp that Richard and Julia had been taken to. Things were getting complicated with the party now split between three locations. We reached the intermediate camp where the porters quickly put our tents up and got dinner prepared. A porter was sent down to the lower camp to tell Richard and Julia what was happening and to make dinner for them. They already had a tent down there. We retired to bed early after an epic day and did not hear Ian being stretchered in at 2am. With all this movement between camps, I never did discover how all the tents and food were moved around as people who should have been carrying equipment were busy stretchering Ian. I suspect that some of the porters had more than one journey between camps in the darkness.

We were concerned about the situation next morning but Ian could walk albeit with very shaky legs and was sent off early with a porter carrying his kit. I must admit that I was feeling so fit and well at breakfast that I ate all the eggs that no-one else could face. After about two hours, we made up on Ian and his strength had almost fully returned. We reached the exit gate without further incident.

Before the climb, in Moshi I had resisted people trying to sell me Kili memorabilia by saying that I could not buy any before I climbed the hill. At the exit gate several miles from Moshi, I was amazed to find three of these peddlers waiting for me – obviously I was too recognisable in the kilt.

When we got back to our hotel, we were presented with certificates recording our individual achievements. I told Ian that the bottom of his should be torn off because he had not done the final section unassisted! After all the porters and guides had given a rendering of the Kilimanjaro song, Ian who is originally from Paisley and myself gave them an impromptu singing of *Flower of Scotland*. I don't think that they had ever had a song in return before and it went down very well.

Naitolia Camp

Because I had travelled a long way to Tanzania, it was only sensible that I should wind down with a safari in the Serengeti and other national parks. This was as wonderful as I had hoped and, in fact, I don't think I could enjoy going to a zoo now.

So, next day, I said goodbye to the Kilimanjaro team and was taken in a Land Rover on a long journey via Arusha to Naitolia Camp in the Tarangire Conservation Area. I was to stay there for several days until another small group joined me for the trip to the Serengeti. Conditions were pretty primitive but very adequate. There was no mains electricity so I just had to hope that my camcorder would last out. All the buildings were built of 3 walls of stone with mesh curtaining on the front walls to keep out the mosquitoes. The roofs were thatched. There was a flush toilet surrounded by walls on 3 sides but the fourth, facing the wilderness, was totally open. The shower was an outside enclosure with a bucket suspended above it with a valve at the bottom, operated by pulling a string. Before breakfast each day, it was filled with water at the right temperature by one of the staff and you pulled the string to get your shower. It was standard practice to have beer or wine available at all meals except breakfast. The tours from the camp, either on foot or, further afield in a Land Rover, were unforgettable with many wild animals being seen.

On one day, I had a rest day so decided to go into Arusha to get some more money and to recharge my camcorder batteries. I was driven to a bus-stop on the main road and, together with our guide, took the mini-bus into town. What a journey. The vehicle had 11 seats in it but, as well as ourselves there were on board 14 adults, 2 children, 1 goat, 1 live chicken, sacks of maize, containers of sunflower oil and many containers of milk. I could not photograph this remarkable scene because I was absolutely wedged against a window. The return journey was a bit better as the vehicle was slightly larger although still very over-laden. However, it was a limited stop service so the trip was far quicker.

On another occasion I had teamed up with a guide and two couples from Australia who had joined me for the trip to the Serengeti. One day, we were taken to a Masai village and told by our guide that we would have to pay money to take photographs of the villagers. We were introduced to the village head-man in his flowing robes whose colours happened to be very similar to those in my kilt. Money for photographs was accepted from the Australians but the head-man pointed at my kilt, gave a thumbs-up, and would take no money from me.

Serengeti and Ngorongoro Crater

After a few days at Naitolia Camp, I was then driven with the two Australian couples over the Rift Valley to the Serengeti. It turned out that our driver and guide, William, had the reputation of being best at finding the animals in the vast spaces of the Serengeti and he certainly proved that with us. The highlight was when he intercepted a pride of lions which crossed our track both in front of and behind us. They were only a few feet away and William had cause to ask me to withdraw inside the sunshine roof as he assured me that the lions and lionesses were good jumpers. At our camp on the two nights we were in the Serengeti, William slept with a rifle beside him and there were constant roarings in the night. I was pleased that they sounded quite distant.

One unexpected event happened. We were travelling in our Land Rover along one of the dirt tracks in the Serengeti when we saw in the distance a people-carrier parked at a strange angle. When we got closer we realised that it had clearly turned over but ended back on its wheels. The engine was dislodged and bits of car were strewn about the road. The only person there was the driver. We learnt later that he had been taking several relatives through the park to a wedding and had lost control. His uninjured passengers had been taken away to find a replacement vehicle so that they could resume their journey whilst he waited for a breakdown truck. When we drove on, our driver said that the man would automatically be fined $50 for having a serious accident in the park. This is a lot of money where the average monthly wage is $20.

Two days later, I was chatting to a Scottish girl at our camp and she told me the full story. Her group had driven past the vehicle which had stopped to change a wheel. Shortly afterwards, it shot past them at a ridiculous speed and just ahead of them, shed the replaced wheel. The car had turned over three or four times. When they stopped to help, they found no serious injuries but quite a bit of bleeding and bruising. The girl told me that there had been a sequel to this the next day. The driver had got a replacement vehicle and succeeded in turning it over in a second accident, again with no serious injuries (another $50 fine). It was then decided that the omens were bad and the wedding had been cancelled.

After three days we travelled on to the Ngorongoro Crater. There is a very steep cliff-side access road to get down into the lush bottom which is full of wild animals. The giraffes never leave the crater because the access track is too steep for such tall animals. Our trip was not without its moments because the brakes failed on our Land Rover and dropping down the steep, rough, cliff-hanging track into the Ngorongoro crater using just the vehicle gears was a nerve-racking experience. Coming up the same track later in the day, we ran out of fuel and other vehicles had to crawl past with inches to spare before one stopped and gave us a 5-litre can of diesel.

After the Serengeti, we were being driven back to Moshi when we again ran out of fuel. The driver had not refuelled after the incident in the Ngorongoro Crater. I got the impression that the travel company was running on a shoe-string but I had got all my promised excursions so was quite happy.

The last journey was to get to the tiny but imposingly named Kilimanjaro International Airport for the return home.

Chapter 5 Asia

5.1 Nepal

I really enjoyed this country which varies from jungle to the world's highest peaks. The people are poor but they all seem to be very cheery and friendly. They love it when outsiders 'bother' to communicate with them.

The Jomsom Trek

I walked from near Pokhara to Jomsom with my two daughters, Julie and Jenny. We took a taxi from Pokhara to the starting point and the taxi had one bump and one near miss, both of which resulted in considerable delays. We could probably have walked most of the way in the same time. When you do eventually get going, the scenery is unbelievable as you actually walk between Annapurna (8,091m) and Dhaulagiri (8,167m) to the north side of the Himalayas. The Kali Gandaki gorge is claimed to be the deepest in the world which is difficult to argue with when the two peaks are more than 3.5 miles above you. I found the scale of things very difficult to accept and, silly though it may seem, the tops gave the impression that they could be climbed in a day. There is just nothing to give the scale of things.

With my daughters on Poon Hill

Partway along the trek is Deorali, a well-appointed village at the top of a pass. About 400m above it is Poon Hill, reputed to be one of the best Himalayan viewpoints. One is recommended to climb it in the darkness and view the sun coming up on the big mountains. Thus, we got up and away before 5.30am in darkness. Many people went back to bed because there was low mist above us. We persevered but, at the summit, were disappointed to see that the big mountains were hidden. Suddenly, just as the sun came up, the mist all disappeared and we had the most magnificent views right round from Dhaulagiri to Annapurna. After enjoying the view for an hour, we went back to our lodge for breakfast. Many people were complaining about missing the view because they had gone back to bed. My lack of sympathy, when I said that in Scotland we knew always to give the weather a chance, did not go down too well.

Shortly after that we had a somewhat alarming experience. We had befriended a local family who were walking home to their village with provisions. All communication was via the young daughter who was learning English at school. My girls and I stopped for a rest and the other family moved on and we saw them passing between two houses on either side of the trail. Men came out of one of the houses and had quite a long conversation with the family which was then allowed to go on its way. We knew that there were troops and Maoists in the area but did not know which these men were. It was claimed that Maoists left tourists alone but who could be sure? It was impractical to turn back as we were two thirds of the way to Jomsom where we had a return flight booked. A vote had me going first whilst my daughters watched to see what happened. No one appeared as I passed the houses so I waved my daughters to come on and we never saw anyone. At the next village, we bumped into the family and asked what it had all been about. They told us that the men were troops looking for Maoists but we would have been recognised as tourists.

The Nepalese people are incredibly friendly especially if you try to communicate with them. We were there at the height of Maoist insurgency having been assured that tourists were absolutely safe. We never had any problems but it was off-putting to round a corner and bump into armed men in plain clothes who might have been soldiers or Maoists.

At one point, we were staying in a lodge and had retired to bed. As I got into my bed, one of my girls asked what was on the wall above my bed. I looked up to see an object, possibly a cockroach but quite large, just above my head. We had walked for a bit that day with an Australian couple and chatted to their guide who spoke good English. I knew he was still up and about so I went to seek him out to ask if the creature was dangerous. He came into the room and said that it might bite and did we have a bag or tissue. I was expecting him to squash it but had forgotten that their religion does not allow them to kill a living thing. We gave him a tissue which he carefully covered the object with and took it out of the room and I followed. We looked into the tissue and there was almost nothing there.

"I don't know where it went," he said, "but it only has 99 legs now."

We flew back from Jomsom to Pokhara. My daughters were rather alarmed on the flight because the pilot was reading a newspaper for much of the journey. We were shocked when, shortly after our return home, the local airline had a crash on that route with no survivors.

Royal Chitwan National Park

Sandwiched between treks we went south to the Royal Chitwan NP for some walks and an elephant trek into the jungle. We did manage to see rhinos, deer, water buffalo and crocs. There were plenty of signs of snakes, bears, leopards and tigers but they were too elusive for us.

When booking various outings at our hotel reception we were told that the hotel had its own elephant and we could go to the lunch-time elephant washing. In fact it was put in the rather strange way of "washing with the elephant." Thus, we met up outside the hotel and I, having been loaded with all the cameras, watched incredulously as my daughters and a Dutch family of four were all loaded bareback onto the one beast. When no mounting platform is available, the elephant is instructed by its mahout to dip its head. You stand high up on its trunk and grab the bottom of its ears and it lifts you right up over its head onto its back where you end up facing the wrong way. You then have a rather tricky manoeuvre to turn round and face the front.

The elephant was then led down to the river whilst I followed using two still cameras and two camcorders. The elephant went straight into the river which was only about a foot deep and proceeded to fill its trunk and spray itself including, of course, its passengers. Julie shouted out that she now understood what was meant by washing with the elephant. Little did she know. The mahout asked Julie to pass down her sunglasses and the question is clearly heard on the video – "Why did he take them?" Next moment, the mahout gave a command and the elephant keeled over and flung everyone into the water after which they were asked to splash water all over the animal. The mahout then invited everyone to climb back on the beast which was on its haunches. Fools that they were, they all got back on, whereupon the beast rose to its feet and keeled over again. Jenny, who was at the front had guessed what might happen and hung onto its ears whilst the others were all pitched into the water.

I took the safe option of riding on its back for the return to the hotel.

Lukla to Namche Bazaar

We had time in hand to trek from Lukla to Namche Bazaar but not, unfortunately, to Everest base-camp. There was tight security at Kathmandu airport and we had to have our luggage searched by very serious staff who had, so it seemed, no sense of humour. I joined the male security queue and my daughters the female one. My daughters got through their security booth quicker than I and when I emerged into the departure lounge, they were in gales of laughter as was a female security person who was coming away from them putting her beret back on. What had happened was that this person had spread the contents of Julie's sack on her desk for a search and then asked Julie to re-pack them. After Julie had emerged into the departure lounge the lady came running after her asking if she had seen her hat. It was found swept into Julie's sack.

The views on the flight from Kathmundu to Lukla are unforgettable but as nothing compared to the landing. One moment, you are hundreds of feet up in the air and the next you have bumped down on the extremely short runway and full reverse thrust is applied. You can see a cliff rearing up at the far end of the runway which is angled up at about 12 degrees. We put out of our minds the takeoff to come a few days later thinking that there would be a great similarity to that from an aircraft-carrier. Actually, I was told that takeoffs and landings were as nothing compared to a few years ago before the runway was tarred!

The two-day walk up to Namche Bazaar was largely uneventful except for one argument that I had with a yak. We came to one of these enormous narrow suspension bridges over a deep gorge and, on the bridge close to the far side was a yak standing facing us. I told the girls to wait while I would shoo it back but it decided to try to push me off the side. It looked worse than it was from where my daughters were standing because I was only about 12 feet above the ground at that point. It wouldn't move but luckily it followed me when I returned to the girls.

The only really hard bit on the trek to Namche Bazaar is the final 600m climb to the village which is exhausting. What did strike me was the enormous loads being carried by porters whilst their clients had small day-sacks. My daughters were carrying day-sacks whilst I had a lot of our stuff in a big sack. I was not in the least bit envious of these other people. In fact, I felt rather embarrassed that the porters were being exploited. There is, of course, the other side to this argument in that I could be accused of depriving the locals of income.

We had a full day ahead of us at Namche and were told that it was well worth climbing 400m up the slope behind the town to the Everest View Hotel, apparently the highest hotel in the world. If we were lucky, we would get excellent views of Everest but we should go early as it tended to cloud over later. Next morning was beautiful and we were away by 06.45 and reached the hotel by 08.30. When we got there, my camera would not work. The battery had run out and I had no spare. I could not believe my luck when I looked at a display cabinet in the foyer and right in the middle of the items was the exact battery for my camera.

The Himalayas were absolutely clear and we had breakfast on the terrace whilst constantly taking in the view with Nuptse, Everest and Lhotse in the centre of a great sweep of glistening mountains. Personally, I thought that the most impressive of the lot was the titchy Ama Dablam at 'only' 6,856m! Cameras and camcorders were going non-stop. My daughters were a wee bit emotional having just read *Into Thin Air* and were now looking over to an apparently very tranquil mountain. We stayed until nearly 10am as the clouds slowly drifted in and hid the high peaks and it was time to go down and visit the weekly market. On the way down, we met several parties going up to view Everest!

We learnt one interesting fact about the weekly market. Some traders travel so far to bring their goods that they start out for Namche before the next market to arrive for the one after that.

We went back to Lukla in one day which was probably a mistake as the route finishes with an uphill and we were exhausted on it. We booked into a hotel right at the airport. It was totally deserted because of the lack of tourists due to the Maoist insurgency. We were led to a large room at the back of the hotel on the top floor and thankfully dumped our sacks on the floor. Julie went to close the curtains and froze. "Dad, could you put the bedside table over the window?" "Why?" I asked. "Come and look," she replied. I did and saw a soldier with a machine gun on a slope behind the hotel. He was just above our

Everest directly above my head from Everest View Hotel

level and no more than 30 metres away and the gun was aimed just over our heads to the runway beyond which he was presumably guarding from terrorist attack. The wooden table would not have been much defence so we just kept away from the window.

We had to clock in at the terminal at 07.00 next morning and, although we were second in the queue, it turned out that the woman in front was holding the documentation for a party of sixteen French. They started to stream in with luggage which they pushed and bumped past us and Julie asked the chap who was obviously in charge to be more careful. He got quite shirty at this and began shouting at us. It was interesting that all the French had their luggage thoroughly searched whilst ours was waved through without being opened. Eventually, we got our boarding passes and went through to the departure lounge. There was a long delay because fog at Kathmandu was preventing planes from taking off from there. Eventually, three identical Yeti Airlines planes came in one behind the other and unloaded. Together with a helicopter, they totally filled the parking area. We had been hoping to get onto our plane first to get window seats on the right-hand side for the best views of the big hills. The three of us and the French party exactly filled a plane and we knew, from seeing one of their group's ticket, that they were on the same plane as us. When the first flight back to Katmandu was called, the Frenchman immediately led his group over to the departure door so we resigned ourselves to the last seats. However, the first plane to be called was not ours and neither was the second. We had to be on the third and last plane and the French leader knew this and moved right up to the door. Now, I think he had been getting up the noses of the authorities and when the door was opened again from the outside, the guard opened the other half of the double door which pushed the Frenchman back and trapped him between the door and the wall. None of the rest of his party would move without him and we simply walked straight past them, trying not to laugh at the nose flattened behind the glass. We got three choice window seats.

I will say one thing in the French party's favour. When we shot off the end of the runway and were clearly climbing, they gave the pilot a round of applause.

A Striking Coincidence

I was travelling home ahead of my daughters and a strike was scheduled for my last three days in Nepal. As all public transport would cease during it, I had to be back in Kathmandu before it started. This would be no great hindrance if we could hire bicycles to explore the city and Kathmandu Valley. We got back to the city on the eve of the strike and I went off in search of the British Embassy to ask if it would be safe to be out and about during the strike. We had been told that the streets would be largely deserted. The soldier at the Embassy gate would not let me past. I tried to persuade him that I was British but he quietly pointed out that it was Easter Monday and the Embassy was closed!

I returned to the centre and decided to get some money out of a 'hole in the wall' in case the machines might run out with no-one to refill them during the strike. I waited in a queue at the machine behind a young lady. Whilst I was carrying out my transaction, I could vaguely hear her speaking on a mobile in the background. She had a Scottish accent. When I had finished I turned round and spoke to her.

"Where are you from?" I asked.

"Scotland."

"Yes, I could tell that from your accent. Whereabouts?"

"Perth."

"Oh. I originally came from Kirriemuir 30 miles away. Are you on holiday?"

"No, I work here."

"Tourism is it?"

"No, I work at the British Embassy and today I am the duty officer."

Out of a population of half a million, I had stumbled on the very person that I wanted to speak to. She was able to tell me that the phone call that she had just taken was to tell her that the strike was postponed for a month.

5.2 Singapore

St. Patrick's Day

I had flown out of Darwin on my way home to the UK and had a 24-hour stopover in Singapore. I realised that it was St.Patrick's Day and I enquired at reception as to whether there was an Irish theme pub in the city. There was, and while I was getting directions to it, an Englishman behind me asked why a Scot was interested in an Irish pub. When I pointed out what day it was, he asked if I minded if he tagged along.

We found the pub and could hardly get in the door as it was so busy. We fought our way to the bar and queued at different points. The English chap got served first and we retired to the centre of the throng to drink. I was shocked to hear that two pints of Murphy's had cost the best part of £14 (it was back in 2000) so we drank slowly. My turn came to get a round and after a ten-minute wait, I returned with the refills. All of this time, a young Irish chap had been entertaining the crowd with songs and guitar. He had apparently been flown over from Ireland especially for this occasion. He stopped for a break and announced that he would leave the sound system on so that anyone could go up and entertain. A couple of Welshmen got up and sang one of their popular rugby songs, *Sosban Fach*, and I thought that it was time for Scotland to do its bit. I had already chatted to two Scottish chaps and I found them again and suggested that we give a rendering of *Flower of Scotland*. They readily agreed and said that they had been chatting to two other Scots and would seek them out. The result was that five of us went up and performed. It brought the house down.

Shortly afterwards, I was nursing my pint when a total stranger came up and asked me if that was Murphy's that I was drinking. When I said "Yes, but slowly because it is pretty expensive," he disappeared and less than two minutes later came back and handed me a pint. When I had thanked him, I asked him how he had got served so quickly. "You've made my day by coming along in a kilt and organising that song. I'm the manager and this is a thank-you." Sometime later as this pint was well down, another stranger came up.

"I hear you're on Murphy's. Here's a pint."

"I know you're not the manager," I said. "Who are you?"

"I'm the Area manager," was the reply.

My English friend interrupted. "I'm going to buy a kilt!"

Chapter 6 Oceania

6.1 New Zealand

This is one of my favourite countries, especially South Island, possibly because it reminds me of Scotland with its mountains, lakes and so many Scottish place names.

Stormy Weather

I had flown into Wellington on North Island and met up with my daughter Julie who was already there on holiday. Next day the ferry left Wellington to make the crossing to Picton on South Island. The public transport services in New Zealand provide excellent running commentaries as journeys progress. It was no surprise, therefore, when the public address system hummed into life as we crossed the bay to go out into Cook Strait.

"This is your captain speaking. Please ensure that you know where sick-bags are stored and stay in your seats as much as possible. It will be slightly windy out in the strait today and the boat will rock a bit in the swell. In fact, you had better hang on tight because we are sailing into a gale."

This was my introduction to the wonderful easygoing attitude in the Antipodes.

Riding the Foot-plate

We were going to travel up the old Taieri Gorge railway from Dunedin in South Island towards Queenstown. Incidentally, the saltire is still flown over the town-hall in Dunedin and all the schoolgirls wear tartan skirts. Large areas of South Island are full of Scottish names but the geography takes a bit of getting used to. For instance, Glenorchy is south-west of Clyde Dam which is next-door to Bannockburn and not far from Roxburgh. When I was in Dunedin, the statue of Robert Burns was getting some maintenance done to it and was totally enclosed by a high fence. Some council official must have seen me trying to peer through the fence to see the statue and saw that I was wearing my kilt. He came rushing out of a building with a key, opened a gate in the temporary fence and gave me a guided tour of the statue.

At the station, there was a large crowd of passengers taking photographs and camcorder shots before we started off. I knew that we were normally allowed out of the train about two thirds of the way through the trip at a large trestle bridge. I went up to the engine driver and asked if there was any chance of riding on the foot-plate from there to the end of the line so that I could get better camcorder shots. He consulted the train manager who said that, unless they were running late, that that would be okay and he would call me at the time.

The train clawed its way up the gorge on a line hanging on the incredibly steep rocky slopes and the views to the depths were absolutely stunning. The feeling of remoteness is very strong because there are no roads in or near the gorge. We crossed many bridges and through several tunnels before eventually stopping short of this enormous trestle bridge spanning a side gorge. We were invited to walk across the bridge so that we could take photographs from the other side of the train coming over. After this, the train manager shouted out that passengers should re-board as quickly as possible but "the chap in the kilt should go up to the engine now."

All photography stopped and heads turned towards me as I walked past to go up to the front and I remarked to no-one in particular that "If you don't ask, you don't get."

Kilt on Ben Lomond

We were in Queenstown in South Island and I, as usual, was wearing the kilt. I was intrigued to see that the nearest hill was the 1,746-metre high Ben Lomond. This just had to be climbed. Forsaking the easier start afforded by a chair-lift to a vantage point above the town, I took the delightful route through the forest and eventually emerged onto the open hillside. There was a chilly breeze which kept me moving along at a good pace. I noticed a couple a little way behind me but one of them eventually turned back. I got to the summit and had great panoramic views including that to The Remarkables as a local range is called. I started to descend and met the single figure coming up. It turned out that he was an Austrian guide on holiday with his wife. He made me feel great when he told

Ben Lomond

me that he had tried but failed to make up on me.

Halfway down, I met an enormous group of Japanese being led up by some local guides. One of the tourists signalled to me asking if he could take a photograph of me in the kilt. When I nodded, he came and joined me while someone else took the picture. Then it happened with another and another..... As each new camera appeared, I started saying "What more?" until the group started chanting "What more?" as well. This went on for about ten minutes and I don't think the group had a clue what it meant but it added two more words to their vocabulary. I eventually left them with much bowing and cries of "What more?" and these cries went on until I was out of earshot. There is no doubt that the kilt brings down barriers world-wide.

I often wonder if the group made it to the summit because, just as I got back to our chalet, the heavens opened and we suffered monsoon conditions for several hours.

Cook's Tour

We had come by the TranzAlpine Express train from Christchurch and bussed down the west coast to Franz Josef village in the hope of getting some good views of Mount Cook. We had been unlucky with the weather when in Mount Cook Village some days earlier. The weather forecast was good for the next day so we booked a half-day tour on the glacier for the morning and decided to take out a mortgage to get a helicopter trip round Mount Cook in the afternoon.

The forecast had been spot on and we had a very enjoyable morning picking our way around and through great fissures on the leading edge of the glacier. It was a trifle cold in the kilt!

In the afternoon came, what to me, was the highlight of the whole trip down-under – the helicopter flight. We were a bit concerned because the mist had descended over lunch. It was a first helicopter flight for both Julie and I and we did not want it to be cancelled or spoilt by poor visibility. We need not have worried. The mist was only above the village and bottom of the glacier and we had soon left it behind. We had been advised to take the helicopter as opposed to a plane for more spectacular views and, by god, they were right. We flew incredibly close to the cliff sides as we gained height towards Mount Cook. Suddenly, it was there ahead of us glistening in the sun. We did a circuit of it at about two-thirds height and could see in the distance Mount Cook Village and glaciers streaming off in several directions. We landed for ten minutes on the top of the Franz Josef glacier but it was so warm in the sun that the kilt was no problem at all. When we came in to land, I reflected on the fact that to climb it, as Hillary did, was a major expedition but I felt, no doubt foolishly, that I could have been dropped off virtually at the summit. Truly, the trip of a lifetime.

Clan Chief

I was in Rotorua in North Island, Julie having remained with friends on South Island. Rotorua is so thermally active that it is nicknamed Sulphur City. I was told that the golf-course has the most interesting bunkers in the world. You do not retrieve your ball from one but have to play a new one. This is because the bunkers are thermal pools!

I decided to go on an evening culture tour to a Māori village where we were to have dinner and I appeared at the designated meeting point in the city in early evening. We were transported out to the village by bus and, for some reason which I never quite clarified but suspected was because I was wearing the kilt, I was appointed clan chief of our bus. I would be personally presented to and welcomed by the village chief as our group's representative. This was to take place in front of the rest of the group. All the pressing of noses (hongi) and sticking out of tongues had to be taken deadly seriously.

I could swear that, as I was welcomed by the chief, there was some sniggering going on behind me but I did feel proud that we were both in national dress.

Auckland Views

I was passing through Auckland at the time of the Americas Cup and had half a day in hand before flying out to Australia. I decided to go down to the Cup Village to see the boats going out on my last morning. Although the boats were not scheduled to leave the harbour until after 10.00 hours, I was advised to get there before 09.00. I got there before 08.00 and the area was absolutely heaving. I asked a guide where I should go for a good view and he directed me to the end of the pier at the harbour mouth. I tried to get there but could not get within 30 metres of the end. As I stood there wondering what to do, the fellow in front of me turned round and, seeing me in the kilt, pushed me in front of him saying "You've obviously come a long way to see this." Within a few minutes, I had been pushed right to the front and had a grandstand view of the boats being towed out right beneath me two hours later. I spoke to the lady next to me and found that she had emigrated from Stirling thirty years before!

I had been aware, while waiting, of the enormous tower in the middle of the city. Spectators told me that it was the Skytower, the tallest man-made structure in the southern hemisphere and open to the public. I thought that, if I went up it, I might see some of the race but, as it turned out, there was not enough wind for racing that day. However, up I went and wandered round the viewing platform 1,100ft. above the streets. At one point on the platform the floor is made up of a large sheet of armoured glass and you are challenged to walk across it. As I stood in the middle of this to take a photograph of the street 1,100ft. below, a voice behind me said "I hope there's no-one looking up from the street at the moment."

Typical Scot

New Zealand has a great ticketing system for booking and paying for journeys by bus, train or internal flight. You can buy a card with so many points on it and each journey costs a number of them. I had bought such a card worth 1,200 points, I seem to remember. On quoting the card number the day before your journey, you are guaranteed a seat and the points on your card are reduced accordingly.

I was nearing the end of the New Zealand leg of my holiday before flying out of Auckland to Australia and trying to ensure that remaining points would get me to Auckland. Eventually, I had one last trip to get there and I phoned up to book it.

The lady on the phone asked me if I was Scottish. When I confirmed this, she said that she had never known anyone to leave a card with only 5 unused points.

6.2 Australia

A land of great contrasts although I was a bit disappointed by one aspect. There is an awful lot of land in the middle with very few points of interest.

Where are the Aussies?

I was on the Wilson Promontory, the most southerly point on the Australian mainland. Out near the point was a small hill, Mount Oberon, and I decided in the extreme heat that a one-hour stroll up it would be quite sufficient. I ambled up meeting lots of people coming down the mainly wooded path. When I reached the summit and its magnificent views over towards Melbourne, there were only six people there. I started to say to them what a fantastic bit of their country this was especially with the almost guaranteed wall-to-wall sun.

They interrupted me. They were Geordies on holiday!

Sydney from on High

A trip in Sydney with the most stupendous views (if you can afford it) is the climb on the Harbour Bridge. Everyone knows what the bridge looks like and the walk goes along the top of the main beam on one side of the bridge up to and across the middle and back down the other beam to the same shore that you started from. You are 440 feet above the harbour in the middle. It has protective railing all the way but what is really cunning is the method

On Sydney Harbour Bridge

used to attach you by a climbing harness and sling to a rail which runs the full length of the climb. A ratchet system gets you past each point where the rail is attached to the bridge frame. What the system does mean is that once attached you cannot change your position in the string of people on the climb so you must persuade yourself to like the people immediately in front of and behind you. You must wear protective clothing and leave behind cameras and all loose objects such as money. Spectacles and sunglasses must be attached to you by a lanyard. An added stipulation is to take a breath test! This is all necessary because of the disaster which could occur if something fell onto a vehicle below. Walking up the main beam is no problem as it is solid steel possibly 4 feet wide. However, when you cross from one side beam to the one on the other side at the very top, you are walking on a mesh flooring which you can see through. Our guide said that, at least once a day, someone freezes at this point and has to be unclipped and led back to the start. The views down to the opera house, city and boats in the harbour are well worth the effort if maybe not the expense.

I learnt one interesting fact about the bridge. The very solid stone buttresses at either end form no part of the integrity of the bridge. They were added as extras because the city fathers thought that the bridge plans as originally presented made it look a bit weak. You start the bridge walk by going partway up inside one of the buttresses and then have to step over a gap which separates it from the bridge's steel framework.

Know the Rules

We were at the campsite at Uluru, otherwise known as Ayers Rock, prior to going to the Rock next day. Incidentally, I got to the top the next day wearing the kilt but was forced to don my good old midge net because of the mossies. I was told that someone the previous year had not only worn a kilt to the top but played the bagpipes there. Anyway, we were sleeping in the open using swag bags which one could describe as sleeping bags with padded bases. Our guide explained that you never get into them before totally unzipping and shaking them out to get rid of any possible nasty insects. However, he said that, although we still had to have our evening meal, we could check the swags now and leave them lying on the concrete plat surrounding the cooking facility. This was because the insects would never venture onto a concrete surface.

As he explained this, I noticed a scorpion approaching him from behind over the concrete and made him aware of the situation. "Dammit," he said as he ground it into oblivion, "I forgot to tell that one the rules."

We all left the checking of our swags till just before getting into them!

Next day, I climbed Uluru which, with hand-rails, made it very straightforward with only one slightly tricky point. On my descent, at this point, there was a drop of maybe five feet and a middle-aged woman was at the bottom of it quietly crying. I asked her what the problem was and she said that she had set her heart on climbing Uluru but it was beyond her. I said that I would get her up this move and the rest of the way to the summit was easy. With all the people on the climb, she would easily get someone to help her down at this point on her descent. I got her over it and that evening I met her in the local pub. She was ecstatic at having made it.

After climbing to the top of Uluru, our group was taken a short distance west to the Olgas. These are very impressive towering rock formations. They looked very hard to climb but, in any case, climbing is banned because they are sacred to the Aborigines. They are so sacred that, apparently, Aboriginal women are blindfolded when in their vicinity.

Snakes Alive

I had gone inland from Melbourne to see some of the country between the sea and The Red Centre and to possibly go up a hill. I found myself in Harrietville in Victoria close to Mount Feathertop (1,922m). It was early afternoon and I enquired locally about going up the hill. I was told that I had probably left it too late to get to the top but I was directed to the start of a path to get me through the dense forest and onto the open hillside. One disappointment in the Australian hills as compared to the Munros is the altitude of the tree-line. In this case, it turned out to be about 1,700m so most of the trip was spent under the thick tree canopy. Before starting, I was also warned to keep to the path and not venture into the undergrowth as snakes lurked there. As a further piece of good news I was told to keep looking around me as some snakes hung around in the tree branches and were apt to drop to the ground.

I started off up the hill in beautiful conditions with plenty of light streaming through the trees. I eventually reached open country and could see the final summit cone ahead with the path clearly going right to the top. Navigation (without a map) would be no problem and I reckoned that I had time to reach the summit and still make it back for a meal. On the final slopes I passed a work-party repairing the path so they have the same erosion problems as we do on popular hills.

The wind had been steadily building up and, as I re-entered the forest on the descent, it had developed into quite a stiff breeze. In addition, a cloud-cover had drifted in and the forest was now quite gloomy. I became a nervous wreck. In the wind, large dead leaves kept slithering noisily down from the trees to the path and I was sure that each one was a snake.

There were no incidents and I finally relaxed with a couple of beers at dinner.

Chapter 7 North America

7.1 South-west United States

My memory of this area is that, outside the cities, it is largely composed of national parks separated by long straight boring roads with the hills on the horizon seemingly never getting any closer.

San Francisco Secrets

Bill and I were doing a sightseeing tour, with some walking thrown in, from San Francisco to Los Angeles and had one day to see some of San Francisco. We did the usual tours to the Golden Gate, Fishermen's Wharf, China Town etc. and were looking for a pub in early evening. We passed a postal worker emptying a pillar-box. Now the town has a bit of a non-heterosexual reputation and I certainly accelerated smartly away when the postman yelled after me for all to hear, "Hey, do you guys wear knickers?"

Shortly afterwards, we bumped into a Scot who was the Scottish & Newcastle rep. for the Western States. He directed us to a pub which sold Scottish beer but there was no suggestion from him of a free handout. He was maintaining a Scotsman's reputation.

Half Dome Encounter

On our tour it was unthinkable that we could by-pass Yosemite. We were, however, disappointed to find that all passes to camp wild in the Half Dome area had been allocated for the next few days. We decided to see how far up the trail by the Nevada and Vernal falls that we could get by starting out early next morning from our campsite in the Valley. As a tribute to John Muir I decided, despite the heat, to wear the kilt.

In fact, there was no problem in getting to the summit of the Dome, via the hawser route, and back down to camp by mid-afternoon.

The final approach to the summit, once you have cleared the woods, is up the steeply angled and smooth dome with the help of two hawsers set up as handrails. Every ten yards or so there are 'passing places', where planks have been attached between the hawser support posts and you can safely pass or overtake at these points.

I waited at such a point to let a chap descending pass me and, in his best

Edinburgh accent, he said, "I should have worn my kilt as well and we could have had a ceilidh here."

Copping it in Lone Pine

We were camping at Lone Pine beside two large recreation vehicles (RVs). We had our wine and steaks laid out on a picnic table when a young chap wandered over from the RVs and introduced himself. The group were all from an extended family and the men were off-duty Los Angeles cops. He went off and came back holding one or two items. To cut a long story short, he introduced me to his version of a Tequila Sunrise. Lemon-juice was squeezed onto salt spread on the back of my hand and I then had to suck it off and wash it down with a slug of tequila. I rather took to it but Bill wisely refrained.

After our meal, we went over and joined them and the drink flowed freely. Bill retired to the tent before midnight but I persevered. At about 2am, we ran out of tequila but one of them hopped into his 4-wheel drive (so much for drinking and driving) and got fresh supplies from the all-night liquor store in the town. We all retired to bed at 05.30.

Bill and I had previously agreed to have an early start at 07.00 to drive into Death Valley to escape some of the heat. I regret to say that I had to leave all of the driving to him.

Death Valley Incidents

Crossing from Lone Pine to Las Vegas, we had come into Death Valley and stopped at an area with the most wonderful golden sand-dunes. We left the car and wandered out onto them and met a chap coming the other way. It emerged that he was a professional photographer from England who had been taking shots at dawn in the dunes. The only problem was that he couldn't find the bulk of his equipment which he had laid down. We searched successfully in the blistering heat and then gave him a lift to Furnace Creek. We wandered into a store which was packed to the gunwales. No-one seemed to be buying – they were simply enjoying the air-conditioning.

Next stop was Badwater, the lowest point in North America, at 280ft. below sea-level. You realise how dramatic the scenery is in these parts when Mount Whitney is less than 90 miles away. It was so hot at 119°F that the car started to boil over and we had to crawl along with the heater going flat out to take the heat away from the engine.

We visited the end of Golden Canyon and I said that I fancied a walk in it. Bill decided to rest at the car whilst I started out. The head of the canyon, which we were told was a remarkable gold colour, was far further than I thought. It turned out to be a round trip of over three miles. On returning towards the car, I met a couple walking in and they insisted on giving me a can of Coke. They pointed out that I had been weaving towards them – a point that, in my overheated state, I had not noticed. They said that, in these conditions, the very most that you should walk without a drink is half to one mile. Lesson learnt.

We exited at Death Valley Junction and we had a remarkable encounter there. We had read that the Amargosa Opera House was there. It was all closed up but we went into the hotel next door for a Coke. We got speaking to the chap behind the bar and said that our guidebook had a very unlikely tale about a dancer whose car had broken down here and she decided to stay, refurbish the opera-house and put on one-person ballet shows. The barman assured us that it was true as she was his wife and "by the way, she's coming in the door now."

She told us that she had been on holiday from New York when she had a puncture in the area and her spare was damaged. Whilst waiting for a replacement, she fell in love with the old opera-house and bought it. Later, she bought the hotel and now did very well from organised tours coming from Vegas for her show and staying overnight. Her repertoire extended to nearly 50 characters and her husband joined her in some of them.

Your Dam Guide

We'd left Vegas, where incidentally I was a winner having gone into a casino with three dimes and come out five minutes later with five plus a free drink served at the one-armed bandit to try to persuade me to stay. We were now taking a tour of the Hoover Dam with a guide who had the somewhat irritating habit of referring to himself as "Your dam(n) guide." I found it interesting that, if left untreated, the Hoover dam will be totally silted up in 200 years. As the tour was finishing, he got the group together and called me to the front. "This man in the kilt will know that there are some big dams in Scotland which I understand to be a fine country. I've shown thousands of people around the Hoover but this is the first ever wearing the kilt. Thank you, sir, for making my day."

Despite our dams at home being put somewhat in the shade by the Hoover, I went away feeling rather proud.

Problems on Route 66

Bill and I turned off Highway 93 onto the famous Route 66 and eventually reached a small town called Selignan in the middle of nowhere. Part of it was done up, or had been maintained, as a wild-west town complete with sheriff's office and jail. Out came the cameras and we wandered down the street, me wearing the kilt.

At the end of the street an RV was parked. It was one of these enormous motorised caravans which you see all over America. As we reached it, a girl came out and asked us if we were from "Scatland."

We got chatting and asked her if she was on holiday. She said that she and her parents lived in North Carolina but had been on holiday in LA and were on their way home. I remarked that that was a long way over the States and would take a few days. Without a word she took me round to the front of the vehicle and pointed to the empty space where the engine should be.

"We've been having a lot of trouble with the engine," she said, "and are waiting for a replacement. We are a sixth of the way home and it has taken us 53 days so far."

Scotland The Brave

Bill and I had just had a great day on Humphrey's Peak near Flagstaff in Arizona. We had now moved onto Williams ready to go to the Grand Canyon the next day.

As we signed in at the campsite, we noticed that a duo was playing Country and Western music in the corner of an outdoor eating area. They must have seen me arriving in the kilt because, when we went in for a meal a little later, they immediately struck up with *Scotland the Brave*.

I went up to thank them and they said that they knew that Scots liked that tune. They said that they never understood why considering that it was a traditional Native American one.

Grand Canyon Mule-trains

If you travel down into the Grand Canyon by foot, you are asked to step to the inside if you meet a mule-train coming the other way. The mules become very restless if placed in a claustrophobic space between people and a cliff face. Incidentally, don't let on that you intend to go down and up in one day as you will be prevented to the point of physical restraint. This is apparently because too many optimists have had to be brought out in wooden boxes. Bill, who was older than me, decided to give the trip down to the Colorado a miss. I took the unofficial advice of starting off in the cool of the early morning and carrying lots of water. I also followed the advice of taking a drink of it every ten minutes before I got thirsty. You cannot drink the running water because of the giardia parasite. Unfortunately, my advisor forgot to mention to me that there is a spring of pure water at the bottom so I need not have carried so much down with me. I was down and up in under seven hours so it is not too arduous for a fit person.

Anyway, I was walking down the South Kaibab trail when I met a mule-train coming up. It was ferrying a group of smiling, chattering Americans back up to the top. I moved in against the steep face and the mules moved right out to the edge of the drop to pass me. The sudden silence and the fixed smiles on the riders' faces was a sight to be seen and never forgotten.

I did wonder why many of the people travelling right to the bottom of the Canyon were carrying only a small rucksack containing a water-bottle. I found out why when I got to the bottom. They had booked canoes or kayaks to travel down the Colorado.

I discovered from other hikers how to keep cooler on the ascent out of the Canyon. You mustn't drink from the streams but you fill your sunhat with water and put it back on. On the way back up, I was approached by a couple at Indian Gardens who asked me what the lower trail was like. They were from Aberdeen!

Powell Point Plouter

We were in Panguitch in the Canyon Country of the States. That afternoon we had tried unsuccessfully to clean our white rental car which was all red to halfway up the doors after a visit to a damp Monument Valley. In the evening we went into a bar and the first thing we heard was that a local woman had just given birth to her twentieth child. The locals said that she had run out of names and had decided to call it 20. "Just the number – she didn't even bother to spell the name."

We asked for suggestions as to where we could go for some hiking the next day. They suggested Powell Point. They explained that it was a great viewpoint along and up some rough roads, which turned out to be similar to our forestry tracks, but that it would be okay in a hired vehicle! They did warn us that there were some shallow ditches over the road and we must be back over them before the routine torrential rain which came for a short spell every afternoon.

We drove as far as we could with the car noting that we had crossed two drainage ditches on the way and then walked the last mile to Powell Point – a marvellous viewpoint over the surrounding countryside. As we walked back to the car we felt a few spots of rain. We ran the rest of the way and started to drive back, breathing a sigh of relief after we had passed the ditches because the rain was getting heavier. Suddenly, the heavens opened and less than a minute later we turned a corner to be confronted by the next hundred yards of road covered by water rushing down the hillside. I shouted to Bill that it could not be deep already and accelerated through it. I was fighting to keep the car aimed at the next bit of exposed road but we made it. When we got back to the campsite, we found that one side of the car had had all the red mud stripped off it. The locals told us that we would have had to wait for at least three hours if we had not charged through the flood.

A flash-flood is a frightening sight.

Angels Landing

We had been exploring the Canyon Country north of the Grand Canyon and came upon Zion. We asked where we might have a short walk in the canyon and, when we confirmed that scrambling would be no bother, the Information Centre guide suggested that we go up to Angels Landing. It was a baking hot day but we did not think we would need water on such a short trip. That was a big mistake!

Angels Landing – approach up the right skyline

It turned out that Angels Landing was an outcrop on a short ridge protruding from halfway up the canyon wall. It was approached by an easy path cut into the canyon wall but the final 150ft. to the top of the crag was very exposed and steel hawsers had been set up as a sort of banister. We got up this stretch and joined quite a crowd on the top and by this stage were pretty desperate for a drink. Judging by the interest, I think my kilt might have been the first one up there. I was approached by a Scandinavian who asked if he could take a photograph of me. Tongue in cheek, I said that Scotsmen usually charged for photos to which he rummaged in his sack and produced a watermelon. He handed me an enormous slice and asked if that would do. On such a scorching day it was worth a fortune.

When we were lazing about, we heard the distant rumble of thunder warning us of the short spell of torrential rain which arrives every afternoon in these parts. As we hurried down using the steel hawsers, we asked a local what one should do if caught in a lightning storm on the top knowing that the aids on the descent were made of metal.

"Pray that your God is looking after you and get the hell out of it," he said.

Cow Country

We were visiting Bryce Canyon in Colorado. It is apparently missed by many tourists who head straight for the Grand Canyon. It is actually only one wall of a canyon and is really an outer wall of the Grand Canyon which is one hundred miles to the south. It should not be missed.

The canyon wall is about 20 miles long and several hundred feet high with many ridges running at right angles to the main face down into the bottom. These ridges are much eroded so that one sees 20 miles of the most weird shapes and the bottom is one large tangle of boulder fields. What is most memorable, however, is that the whole lot is bright orange.

The first person to try to eke out an existence under the cliffs was a Scotsman called Ebenezer Bryce. When he had been there for several years someone asked him how he was getting on. "Aye, nae bad," he said, "but it's a hell of a place to lose a coo."

Joshua Tree National Park

We were returning to the coast at San Diego and stopped one night at Joshua Tree National Park. The Joshua Tree is so called because it is meant to resemble Joshua waving his arms about when giving a sermon. We pitched our tents and then went for a drive round the park. Signs directed us to a viewpoint on a small knoll which had some information displays. I looked out and said to Bill "I wonder what that groove is out in the wilds about 200 yards away." Bill looked at an information board and said "It's the San Andreas Fault!"

The Queen Mary

Long Beach, California, and the good old Queen Mary had to be visited. The grand old lady really has been kept in immaculate condition, still floating but surrounded by a protective breakwater. Being an engineer, I especially wanted to see the engine-room but it was out of bounds due to filming – probably some Bruce Willis epic. Even wearing the kilt, no amount of pleading that I had come thousands of miles from Clydeside to see it would help. I resigned myself to a wander round the rest of the ship.

There was a brass quintet playing mainly jazz out on deck. As I approached, they abruptly changed tune to Amazing Grace and one of them shouted out "Just for you, Scotty."

Santa Monica Highlights

Before flying home, we were staying for a few days with friends in Marina Del Rey just north of LA. They recommended two visits to us – the Museum of Flying and the John Paul Getty museum both in Santa Monica. The latter has now moved to a much larger site.

We went to the Museum of Flying first. There was plenty of interest including a plane, Japanese I think, which had a rear engine driving a propeller at the front. This gave plenty of view to the front but was unpopular with the pilots because they sat astride the drive-shaft. A broken drive-shaft did not bear thinking about. We had to ask an attendant if they had anything on Concorde and he showed us a three inch model of it. They keep quiet about it over there. He further annoyed us by insisting that Charles Lindbergh was the first man to fly the Atlantic. We pointed out that his was the first solo flight but that Alcock and Brown had made the first one. He just would not accept that.

Our guidebook said that we should see Spitfires but we could not find them anywhere so I approached another attendant to ask. He answered with a Scottish accent. He had been born in Forfar at the same nursing-home as myself, had flown Spitfires and had lived in the States for many years. He said that the museum had two Spitfires but they were in their workshops being spruced up for the following flying season. "Would we like to see them?" The museum is on the edge of a private airfield and the workshops were at the far side. The next thing, he was driving us over the runways under control tower directions to the hanger. The two Spitfires were in wonderful condition and the mechanics were thrilled to show us around. They had nothing but praise for their flying performance.

Our next stop was to be the John Paul Getty museum and we found that it was at the north end of a beach cycle-track which ran from Redondo Beach in the south. We knew that parking at the museum was very difficult because of complaints of indiscriminate parking from householders in nearby streets. You either had to pre-book one of the very limited spaces at the museum or produce a bus ticket to prove that you had come by public transport. We decided to cycle there and see whether we could get in. The cycle up on a track on the edge of the beach was amongst all the beautiful people jogging, roller-blading, cycling etc., and there were certainly plenty of them. One of them so engrossed me that I cycled off the track into the sand and went straight over the handlebars. It was one of the few times when I was wearing shorts instead of the kilt! We got to the museum and there was no problem despite our somewhat casual appearance. The gate-man tucked the bikes round the back of his booth.

We planned, after leaving the museum, to cycle right to the south end of the track at Redondo Beach and then back to Marina Del Rey, a total distance from the start of the day of 15 to 20 miles or so our friends assured us. We eventually got to the south end where there was a large queue of joggers at a telephone booth. We asked what it was all about to be told that they were phoning for their other halves to come and pick them up. We were rather tired when we eventually got back to Marina Del Rey where we found that our trip of 15 to 20 miles was actually 45. So much for the estimate of our electronics engineer friend!

7.2 The John Muir Trail

This trip was conceived in a Berber tent in Morocco and lived up to all expectations. A major difference from Morocco was that there were no mules to carry the loads. Carrying up to 45 pounds weight when you are over sixty is hard but the virtually guaranteed weather is a delight.

Permits

Four of us got together to organise a trip to California to trek the John Muir Trail along the Sierra Nevada. You are only allowed into the wilderness if you have the necessary permits for each of the National Parks on the route. These passes are much sought after and those for any starting week are made available 23 weeks in advance. They can be booked by 'phone or email and, as I was retired, the group handed me this responsibility. The relevant advance period arrived and there was no problem in booking by email and I had my confirmation through the post from the Yosemite Valley Rangers a few days later. About two weeks later, a fifth person asked to join us. I phoned up the Rangers and explained the situation. When they learnt that we were coming from the UK they said that they would bend the rules which did not normally allow additions to numbers. I received a further confirmation. Another two weeks later, a sixth person wished to join us. Somewhat in trepidation, I phoned Yosemite again. I got hold of the same chap and he said that he could not change the numbers again but that he would hold back one of the limited passes handed out each starting day. I said that this was too risky for someone coming thousands of miles.

"Gee," he said. "I love your Scottish accent. You've got your sixth pass."

Supplies

The JMT is over 225 miles if you take in diversions to Half Dome and Vermilion Valley Resort, an excellent place for a rest day. Not many people are capable of carrying at least 18 days' supply of food on top of all their other gear, especially as the food has to be stored in quite heavy bear barrels. These containers, which are compulsory and bear-proof, can be hired at Yosemite. Food, however, can be posted ahead to four locations, albeit all in the first half of the Trail. We did not know about the fourth drop point so carried more than necessary on one section.

We had brought quite a lot of dehydrated food with us and were surprised that we had had no problems at Customs given that there was a foot-and-mouth epidemic at home. We took the train from San Francisco to Merced and found our pre-booked hotel. The remainder of our supplies were bought in Merced and we then had to sort them into parcels for posting ahead. Kim, who is quite an expert in these things, had drawn up menus comprising dehydrated food, oat-cakes, tubes of pâté and cheese, biscuits, energy bars, tea-bags etc., for each day. We ended up with a hotel bedroom floor covered with masses of packets as we sorted out the team's requirements for each of our planned 20 days. This was all incredibly detailed because, to cut down on weight, things were planned and counted out to the individual tea-bag, oat-cake, energy bar, drink sachet etc. These then had to be bundled into parcels to be posted ahead as well as retaining that required for the first leg. Fuel supplies had to be organised in the same way although we knew that some of that could be replenished from two or three stores en route. We cut out some weight by sharing two-man tents and having one set of cooking equipment per pair. Nevertheless, each of us had a base load of about 14kg without food. The longest leg without a re-supply point is the final 110 miles and we found that we started that section with loads of about 21kg. I can assure you that for someone over sixty that was heavy. However, the younger ones in the party found it no easier. To get our rucksacks onto our backs, we had to prop them up on rocks and reverse into them.

Organising food for the JMT

We had all our parcels ready for posting late on Friday night and went round to the Post Office on Saturday morning. It was closed on Saturdays. We could not delay posting because our first food-parcel pickup was less than four days away. Also, we could not delay our start because you must leave Yosemite Valley on the stated day or you forfeit your passes. Eventually, we discovered that there were alternative postal services and we found one open. Last minute panic over.

We all found the loads heavy despite our efforts to keep the weight down. At a food pickup point a week later, we found that they would accept outgoing parcels. We jettisoned almost all of our spare clothing, binoculars, reading material etc. and posted it ahead to a hotel in Lone Pine. We learnt that you have to be absolutely ruthless in what you pack.

Eve of Starting

We had checked in with the Rangers, collected and packed our bear barrels and were camped in Yosemite Valley in the free area set aside for people doing the trek. A hearty last meal was called for before weeks of a strict diet. We had a good meal at Curry Village and were wandering back to our campsite beyond the main one. Alan, who had taken some ribbing because of the socks with a Donald Duck motif that he was wearing, suddenly decided that he wanted to go to the toilet. He ran ahead and shot into the toilet-block. When we neared it, we realised that he had gone into the ladies' half. We were about to shout into him when three girls approached and went to go in. We explained what had happened and asked them if they would mind us going in the door with them whilst we told him what he had done. We all went in together and could see, under a toilet door a pair of socks adorned with Donald Duck. David shouted out what Alan had done, amid girlish laughter. Not a sound came from the cubicle but a pair of trainers surmounted by Donald Duck socks lifted slowly out of sight. Eventually, when the girls had gone, we shouted that the coast was clear and he scurried out before anyone else appeared and trapped him in his trap.

Funnily enough, when we had our first get-together after we got home, it turned out that his wife, Beryl, who had not been on the trip, said that she had heard many tales from Alan about the trip but not that one.

Bare, Bear Necessities

On the first day, three of us were going better and pulled ahead. We all wanted to do the four-mile round trip diversion to take in Half Dome. We would all meet up at Half Dome junction, padlock and leave our sacks together and go up the Dome with no loads. The three of us waited at the junction but when the others appeared, they had no sacks. They had left them 900ft. lower at the wrong junction. We climbed Half Dome in blistering heat and were very tired by the time that we got back to the junction where we had left our sacks. We had planned to camp near here but, after a discussion, decided that we would have to split our camping that night. Those of us with our sacks up here did not want to go down 900ft. and those with sacks at the bottom felt that they could not go down and back up with heavy sacks the same evening. They camped down in Little Yosemite Valley.

There had been talk of bears in our wild spot the night before so we used our rope to sling some of our food from the trees. The bear barrels could not accommodate it all. The ones who had descended to camp lower down had no rope so left their sacks outside their tent. We had kept two tents at our upper camp and the three at the lower camp were squeezed into one tent. In the early morning, a noise wakened them and David went out to investigate. He shouted that there was a bear rolling his sack down the slope. He yelled at it and it eventually ambled off.

In the meantime, Kim told Andy to go out and help.

"I can't," he said.

"Go on you wimp," said Kim.

"I can't," he repeated, "because I've got nothing on."

This story was also repeated at a get-together after the trip and Andy's partner, who had joined us, turned to him and said "You never told me the last bit!"

The Lost Food-parcels

Our first food drop was to be at Tuolumne Meadows only two or three days after we started out and we did not want to risk posting the two parcels in case the delivery was late. We had phoned Yosemite Rangers from Merced and they had said that they would take them round from Yosemite to Tuolumne Meadows by road. When we got to Tuolumne Meadows, we could not find them anywhere – the Wilderness Centre, the Ranger Centre, the store, the Post Office, the campsite office or the Lodge. We phoned Yosemite and they had left there but the person bringing them had now gone into the wilderness for several days. The upshot was that we had an enforced rest-day early on in the trek and we only had two spare days in total. More frantic phoning on the rest day was getting us nowhere although the whole Ranger Service seemed to know about our predicament. We were resigned to buying food in the local store but the US dehydrated food was considerably heavier for the same energy content as the UK supplies. Total strangers were incredibly kind and were offering us spare food and we were about to use these various facilities to build up our supplies. On the way to the store, a Ranger intercepted us. The parcels had been left at El Portal by mistake. A special run was being made to bring them up to Tuolumne. They eventually arrived at 5pm and we got ourselves sorted out for an early start next day.

The lost day put a strain on our timetable but what was so memorable was the absolute kindness of everyone in trying to help us. Possibly, the kilt helped – who knows?

The Water-carrier

We had kept to our planned timetable after Tuolumne but had been very lucky going up the Lyell Canyon. There had been a violent thunderstorm on our rest day and lightning had started a fire high on the opposite slopes of the canyon. We had seen the small fire as we walked the canyon. Apparently, such fires are normally left to burn out because helicopter water-drops can cause severe erosion. A few days later, the sky away behind us went very hazy. The fire had got out of control and that section of the John Muir had been closed. If we had not passed it in time, we would never have completed the whole trek.

We were now at Devils Postpile, a feature similar to the basalt columns at Fingal's Cave on Staffa. The brochure actually mentions Fingal's Cave and the Giant's Causeway as being the other two best examples of the feature. Because it is a National Monument it has been made accessible to motor traffic. We were thus camping that night in a typically noisy campsite. I took all of our water containers to fill at the water supply-point whilst the others put up the tents. On the way back, loaded up with about a dozen bottles, a chap drinking beer outside his RV got chatting to me and asked what a fellow wearing the kilt was doing in these parts. When I explained, he remarked that it must be tiring and gave me a can of cold beer. I saw little point in sharing it with my five colleagues so it was finished before I got back to them. The usual comment of "You and your kilt," ensued and they rather half-heartedly said that they weren't interested in a beer anyway.

Close-by to the Devils Postpile is Reds Meadow Resort. We found two marvellous energy-boosters there. Hot thermal springs, where we got our first washes in hot water since Tuolumne, and a store which served great meals. The resort now accepts food-drops despite what our guidebook said. We even found a public 'phone box to 'phone home from.

Meeting People

I have not mentioned the continuous wonderful scenery as that is well covered in other literature. However, over and above that, what I especially enjoyed was the conversations with others on the trail. On many occasions, I was likened to John Muir because of my beard and the kilt, of course, which placed me firmly in Muir's native land. He is a national hero out there because of what he did for National Parks; whereas, when I was there in 2001, he was little known in his homeland. Everyone on the Trail seemed to have a Scottish ancestor. Actually, some were Irish but we'll gloss over that. In addition, word had got ahead that we were coming and the Rangers down the trail and people walking the other way were all expecting us. It made the whole trip so incredibly friendly and added another layer of enjoyment.

I think, especially, of Big Al who was well into his eighties and walking the Trail for about the tenth time. Every time that he finished, he would say that that was the last but he came back year after year.

Then there was Linda who had started out with a walking companion who had developed an injury and had to drop out. She joined us for about half the trek and we left her near the end where her husband was to walk in with food next day. When we compared notes by email after we got home, we found that we had eaten in the same place in Lone Pine two hours apart.

On one occasion, Alan and I were well ahead of the others on Forester Pass near the end of the trek. We were joined by an off-duty Marine Reserve and his uncle. We were getting short of food and they plied us with biscuits, paste and sweets, some of which we saved for the others. However, we didn't tell the others until the trek was over how much food we actually got that day.

Most people going our way were keeping to our sort of pace and it was most enjoyable constantly meeting 'old friends'. We met many of them again in Lone Pine where we spent three days after we had finished.

The Ranger Station

We were on the third last day and running desperately short of food. Someone on the trail had told us that the Ranger-station at Crabtree often had spare food left behind by people who had come down from Mount Whitney. It was another glorious day and there was a lot of lounging around. I slowly pulled ahead and found the station which was a short way down a well-marked diversion. I just hoped that the others coming behind would read the diversion sign. The Ranger was in residence and, when I tentatively mentioned spare food, she invited me in and pulled out two large boxes of goodies.

By the time that the others arrived, I was tucking into biscuits and cheese, chocolate and fruit juice out of a sachet. She looked on in absolute amazement as everyone dived into the boxes and came out with treasures. All of our supplies problems except one were instantly solved. The last was fuel. We actually squeezed our last breakfast two days later out of the last can of fuel. Another night on the hill and it would have been a cold dinner.

The Finish

Strangely enough, the official finish of the Trail is the summit of Mount Whitney (14,491ft.) but the recognised ending is at the end of the public road at Whitney Portal 6,000ft. below. If you don't have transport waiting there, you then have to get down to Lone Pine on the junction with the main freeway up the east side of the Sierras. This journey is 13 miles on tarmac so we were looking for lifts. We reckoned that we would never all be given a lift at once so we split up and wandered around the parking lot. Almost immediately, I got a cry of "Hey Scotty, we saw you on the summit yesterday. Want a lift to Lone Pine?" I told the others that I had got a lift, said I would try to get a hotel and arranged to meet them 'at the traffic-light'. We had learned that everything in Lone Pine seemed to centre on this one set of lights called 'the traffic light'.

On the summit of Mount Whitney

I was soon down in Lone Pine. The two chaps in the car actually, to the envy of my mates, gave me a tour of the Alabama Hills which are partway down the road. These hills have appeared in just about every western which does not feature Monument Valley. In Lone Pine, I wandered around various hotels and got us a tremendous deal at one right next to 'the traffic light'. It turned out that the movie stars, including John Wayne, had always made this hotel their base in town. The others took over two hours to join me by which time I was making up for lost beer-drinking.

Later in the day, as we wandered around the town, there was the most dramatic and violent thunder and lightning storm over Mount Whitney. We would never have made it to the top if we had been near the summit at that time because notices on the paths forbid you from going up in these conditions.

Half the town seem to be expecting us and we got great welcomes wherever we went. It turned out that many Americans do the Trail in separate legs over the years and the locals did not meet so many people who had done the full trek in one go. As well as 225 odd miles to walk, the uphill totals over 45,000 feet.

On our last evening in Lone Pine before going to LA for the flight home, some of us went out on the town. We went into one bar which was just about to close and persuaded the barmaid to serve us a couple of drinks. We found that, outside cities, bars tended to close in mid-evening. I wandered over to the jukebox and soon had us dancing to *By Yon Bonnie Banks*. The bar then closed up but we were directed over the street to a bar that "sometimes stayed open later." We went in and it was about to close. There was no problem in getting the barman to keep it open for an hour. His father had been born in Govan!

Oh, what a small world!

Postscript

When we got home, my wife Eleanor had one look at my kilt and said that it was for the bin. It had almost been worn through at the back by the constant rubbing from my enormous rucksack. It's a wonder that I was not apprehended by the authorities for indecent exposure after the walk had ended. Back in Scotland, it was replaced very quickly as I had no intention of using my dress kilt on the hills.

Chapter 8 Hill Access and Other Things

Access to the hills

In the main, the comments that I make here regarding access apply in Scotland as I have less experience of the situation elsewhere. You may well disagree with the whole concept of people going out to shoot wild-life. Nevertheless, coming from Angus, I am well aware of how important this income is to the wellbeing of estates. I have therefore always tried not to upset these activities.

Over the years, I have had very few run-ins with keepers by sticking to a few simple self-imposed 'rules'. In the main, grouse moors have not been a problem because I tend to have been operating at a higher altitude. Keepers have also told me that walkers do not pose much of a problem in the hind season because it is not a case of stalking an individual selected animal. I have, however, been addressed in an aggressive manner in the hind season but politely put my point of view and retired or gone on, depending on how the conversation went. During the stag season, when the appropriate older or injured animals are selected for culling, a walker or climber can spoil hours of preparatory tracking by blundering into an area.

During this season the simplest solution is to visit areas which have no stalking. However, if I really want to walk in a stalking area I try to make it on a Sunday when, by tradition, no stalking takes place. At other times I take advice from the outdoor access website *Heading for the Scottish Hills* or I ask at the local keeper's house. If I cannot find where the keeper lives I look for estate vehicles on or near the hill that I want to climb. Vehicles are a sure sign that they are out there somewhere. If, after all of this, I do meet a party on the hill, I explain what I have tried to do and this is normally well received although I might be asked to modify my planned route.

The occasion where keeping on good terms with keepers is really useful is where access to remote hills can be eased. Keepers such as Duncan Maclennan or Geordie Oswald would leave a key at a prearranged location or give the number to open a combination lock on a locked estate access road.

Once or twice, I have got the appropriate okay from someone on the estate to be confronted later by another estate worker on the hill. On one occasion, having got the okay from 'the big house' to take my car up a private estate road, I returned to it to find it blocked in by a Land Rover. I had to wait two and a half hours for the keeper to return. I explained the situation to him but he informed me that only he took such decisions. Perhaps I should have taken that point up with the estate owner. Most keepers will be appreciative when they hear what action you took before going on the hill. Some are just bloody-minded but, especially now that we have freedom of access legislation, they are, in my experience, in the very small minority. I have found that the owners tend to be more understanding and a quiet comment to the keeper that you will mention the meeting to the owner tends to calm things down. In this day and age, estates do their best to facilitate hill people and we, in turn, should remember that they have a living to make. When I have sought and been given permission to drive onto an estate, on several occasions, the keeper has told me not to go any further with my car because the estate road is in poor condition. He has then driven me further in using an estate vehicle.

Incidentally, I have heard that, in England and Wales, estate workers can be more aggressive. I have of late being climbing smaller hills in these countries and make a point of asking for access at local farms. I have been refused only twice. In each case, I was told that I could not go up a particular hill, one in Wales and the other in England. On both occasions, I was told that I might upset the lambs. Both times I then drove round and climbed the hill from the other side and there was not a sheep or lamb in sight.

Navigation

There is no doubt that GPS technology has been a great help to navigation in the hills. When I am planning a route, I try to set waypoints so that the route between any two is relatively straightforward. However, I always take map, compass and spare batteries with me. No electronic kit is totally foolproof and, in thickly wooded or steep-sided areas, the GPS signal can be lost. It seems to be becoming more common to rely totally on maps on mobiles for navigation. When I ask people navigating by such means if they also have map and compass, I am often informed that they are not necessary in this modern electronic age.

I once had a concerning experience in the hills. I was climbing quite a low hill and fields of deep bracken were all over the hillside. As I ascended, seeking out clear patches around the bracken, I set waypoints so that I could avoid the bracken on the descent. Just as I set the last waypoint before the summit, I was enveloped in a violent snow storm and visibility was reduced to a few yards. I decided to exit the summit fast and selected this last waypoint. I could just see my tracks faintly in the falling snow but the GPS was pointing well to the left. I followed the arrow for a minute or two but could see no sign of my foot-prints. I stopped and selected the second last waypoint which took me in the right direction. Had the signal for the last way-point been corrupted by the falling snow?

In the days before GPS, I used one or two techniques which helped navigation in misty conditions. On one particular hill, a Land Rover track stops several hundred metres short of a fence which goes right to the summit. There is no problem in taking a compass bearing from the end of the track to the fence and a reverse bearing will get you back to it. The problem is that you have to know where to leave the fence on the descent. What I did was to hack off the fins of ice on the fence wires at the point where I met it. I just had to look for this point on the descent.

Many tracks have numbered power-cable poles leading to remote houses. If I was using a bike on the track but had to leave it to cut across to a hill, I would leave the bike at a pole, note the pole number and whether these numbers were ascending or descending from pole to pole. Then, when I returned to the track, I knew whether to turn left or right to find the bike.

I have known a party of us on undulating ground going 180 degrees out in a few minutes when busy chatting instead of navigating. We have been known to spot footprints in the snow beside a lochan and remark that we must be on the right track only to realise it is our own footprints from a few minutes before and we had walked all the way round the lochan. Navigation, especially in inclement weather, requires constant concentration.

On one occasion, I was given advice on how to navigate a route which was more a climb than a scramble. It was to follow the Javelin Jacket wool caught on the rocks. This advice was spot on!

Transport

Bikes are an obvious form of transport in getting to remote hills. Many places have good forestry or estate tracks. However, punctures are always a possibility and can be hard to deal with in inclement weather. I always carry a spare inner tube with me to avoid having to do repairs. However, I do remember on one trip to Bendronaig Lodge to climb Lurg Mhòr and its neighbour that I had one puncture and my companion two. Then there is the story, told elsewhere in this book, of my experience with collapsed chain-rings on the approach to Mount Keen. Several times I have had a chain snap with a damaged link and have had to resort to a shorter chain fixed in one gear to get me home.

The car is normally a pretty safe form of transport. However, on one occasion, when we came off a hill south of Braemar, the car just would not start. We did not know the phone number of the garage in Braemar so we had to push it there and it was about three miles. The garage got it working again for the next morning.

On a hot and sweaty day, I pulled ahead of my companions on a climb of An Socach south of Braemar and was dozing in the sun when they arrived. "Did you speak to your visitor?" they asked. When I looked baffled they explained that a hang-glider had passed over me at no great height. There have been times, especially on a hard day in the hills, when I have thought that the descent of the last hill would be much easier by hang-glider. The alternative thought was to consider asking to be 'beamed down by Scotty'.

Weather

Over the years, I have learnt much about weather conditions and what you can do to ease the situation. There is a weather condition known by my friends as 'Logan's blue sky'. This comes from my observation of even the smallest patch of blue sky appearing which might indicate that better weather is coming.

In very windy conditions, it makes a big difference in the hills if you can choose an ascent which is sheltered from the wind for as long as possible. On many occasions I have managed to keep in the lee of a hill until well up to the final summit ridge. In these conditions in winter do not delay putting on crampons until you are in the middle of an icy slope with the winds tearing at you. I remember on one hill near Loch Tay when two of us put on our crampons quite low down when the snow was not especially hard. However, we got to the summit despite the gale. Another group from our climbing club left it too late. They had to descend when they could not get their crampons on in the higher icy conditions.

Be prepared for the unexpected. I have met a double cornice on the South Glen Shiel Ridge. I would never have got across without the aid of an ice-axe to allow me to slowly move forward whilst prodding for overhangs. We have sensibly turned back on Tower Ridge on the Ben when hit by snow in early September when not prepared for the possibility. One should also heed all the advice about carrying layers of clothing so that they can be put on or taken off as conditions change.

In inclement weather, try to choose a route avoiding sizeable burns with no bridges. These can involve considerable detours upstream or, if that is not possible, a retreat. Try to learn about the effect of persistent rain in an area when making your plans. A good example is the Fisherfield Forest where rivers can rise at an alarming rate. It can be a couple of feet in a very short time. There used to be one strand of an old bridge still remaining on the route from Shenavall bothy to Ruadh Stac Mòr. I have a photograph of one of my mates coming hand over hand over the single wire. The water is about 4 feet below him. I have come over that wire when the water was trying to tear the sack off my back. Two things can help on a river crossing – walking poles or a bike to lean on. I remember going up Ben Klibreck from the north and the river at the bottom was quite easy to cross. When I came down two hours later, the river was impassable and I only got over where a high shaky fence crossed it. A friend had tried to cross at the same place two or three years before and dropped his ice-axe in the middle of the operation. It got swept into the loch and was lost.

A totally different experience where forward planning is needed due to tidal effects is The Chain Walk near Elie in Fife. This is a ledge at the base of a cliff just above the water and there is a chain to hang onto. Attempt it at the wrong tidal conditions and you will be trapped and not able to get off at either end.

Reducing Dangers

My first advice would be that, when you are out on hills of any significance, you always take a map and compass and know how to use them. Do not rely totally on electronic navigation equipment but do take spare batteries with you.

There is plenty of advice available as to what clothing to wear and equipment and spare clothing to carry for various weather conditions. That advice comes from many years experience so learn from it.

Especially if you are travelling solo, get as much information as you can about your planned route before going. Assess that the route is within your capabilities especially if the forecast is for poor weather. Leave someone, at home or locally, with details of your planned route. Personally, I am always reluctant to leave route details in the car because of the danger of inviting a break-in.

Do not let your concentration drift in tricky situations. Remember that simple trips or falls could result in a serious situation. A twisted ankle many miles from civilisation, especially in the winter, can be life threatening.

If more of your experience is of summer conditions, even if you have been out in poor conditions in really foul weather, remember that the conditions in winter can be much more serious.

The two photographs here show the same chimney in the Crazy Pinnacles on the Aonach Eagach in summer and winter.

Aonach Eagach chimney, summer and winter

There are plenty of hand-holds in summer conditions but the winter conditions mainly require the use of axe and crampons and the knowledge of how to use them properly.

I have already mentioned one tragedy on An Teallach where the cause might well have been one of the people involved operating beyond their capabilities. On another occasion, we were staying in a climbing club hut in mid-winter when a stranger arrived. He told us that he was a member of the club that owned the hut and asked if we could allow him to wait inside whilst someone came to pick him up. We, of course, welcomed him and, as he was a bit subdued, asked if there was a problem. He told us that he had been walking up the south-east ridge of Bidean nam Bian with a mate. They stopped for a breather at a small stance half way up. He turned one way to see the view and, when he turned back, his friend had disappeared. He spotted him lying at the bottom of a cliff on the north side of the ridge. When the rescue services reached him it regretfully turned out that he was dead. The stranger had no explanation as to what had happened. It had all occurred within a few seconds which clearly indicates that danger can be lurking close by.

On another occasion, a party of us had walked up the traditional tourist route to the summit of Ben Nevis. It was white-out conditions with the path totally hidden by snow so that we reached the summit on compass bearings. We went into the survival shelter which sits on top of the old observatory ruins and joined two chaps already in there having their lunch. It turned out that they were from Ireland and were staying at the Youth Hostel down in the glen. We left them and descended back to Fort William in appalling conditions.

Next day news came that two Irishmen who were staying at the hostel had fallen down Five Finger Gully to their deaths. It would have to be an incredible coincidence if it was a different pair from the two that we had spoken to. I have often wondered if they did not know that, on leaving the summit of the Ben, you start off on one bearing then have to turn sharply onto another just above the gully. Did a lack of pre-planning lead to their demise?

In summary, do as much forward planning as possible but always be on guard for the unexpected.

Animals

We have had a few unplanned encounters with animals in our travels.

Red deer stag

On one occasion, we were travelling in separate cars up to Skye and Donald never appeared. We got his story when we arrived home. He had just left Bridge of Orchy in the darkness and was on the long sweeping bend going up to the Blackmount when a stag leapt into the road ahead of him. He couldn't avoid it and it cracked his radiator, slid up his bonnet and smashed the windscreen before leaving a bloody and scratched mess over the roof and down the boot. His insurance company took a lot of persuading that all the damage had been caused by the one incident.

On another occasion, Kenny was driving us up the A9 to Torridon when a deer came out of the darkness on the left. Kenny swerved left to miss it but it turned back and there was the most almighty thump. We stopped to investigate the damage and those on the near-side of the car could not open the doors – all the body-work had been pushed back. We were stopped shortly afterwards by a patrol-car for having a headlight missing but were allowed to go on our way when we explained the circumstances.

When we were at a bothy in the West Highlands, one of the Club members decided to have a go on the back of a garron in the field. When he got astride, it bolted towards a dry-stane dyke and stopped abruptly sending said member right over the wall. Only his pride was hurt.

Two of us were driving up a side-road to some obscure hills. The road was sunk between high bankings. There were no animals in sight but suddenly a sheep leapt from the top of the banking and the car hit it before it reached the ground. Its wool protected both it and the car and it wandered away apparently unharmed. Round the very next corner, we came upon the shepherd pushing animal-feed out of the back of a Land Rover.

I had cycled up Glen Lochay one day to climb Beinn Heasgarnich and Creag Mhòr. When I returned to the locked gate at the end of the public road, a muckle great bull stood by it. It just stared at me and I was obliged to carry the bike 50 yards up the hillside and over the fence to avoid it.

The Demon Drink

Our Club has been known to enjoy a tipple. Some years back Chris, who had joined us for a summer whilst he was seconded to Scotland, returned back south. He was talking to someone in a pub who, it turned out, had gone out with our Club a few times. They compared notes and realised that they had both had a spell with us.

"How did you get on with them," Chris asked the other chap.

"Fine," he replied, "but they do like a drink, don't they?"

Then there was a famous occasion in a climbing hut when one member had indulged in too much Southern Comfort and was getting a bit obstreperous. This was not sensible in someone else's abode so we solved the problem by tying him to a chair with a climbing-rope.

A young chap joined us and could not hold his drink. He was put outside until he cooled off. Someone went out later to check that he was okay as it was a cold evening. He was found fast asleep on top of the coal in the coal-shed. The experience sobered him up and we had no further problems with him.

In his younger free and easy days, before he got married and settled down, another member staggered out of the front-door of one hut, rolled down a banking and became tangled up in a barbed-wire fence. That was a very effective way of sobering up.

After a particularly boisterous night at the Clachaig in Glen Coe, we retired to our tents. In the morning, one of the party groaned that he would not manage out. The other two of us went up Bidean and returned to the tents in mid-afternoon. Our mate was still not up and, when we looked into his tent, he was fast asleep lying on top of his emergency supply of cans of beer. Back in the pub that evening he stuck to orange-juice.

On one occasion, we were staying in one of the self-catering outhouses at Kinloch Castle on Rùm. We had joined another group in their building for the evening leaving the windows in our bedrooms open because it was quite muggy. One of our party went to bed early and shut the window in his bedroom. We had with us for the first time a young chap and, early in the evening, he remarked that we did not seem to drink much. He appeared to try to drink on behalf of the rest of us and went to bed slightly the worse for wear in the same room as the chap who had retired earlier. As soon as he reached the room, he felt very ill and rushed to the window to be sick not realising that it was closed. The result was that he was violently sick in the room. He opened the window ready for the next time and, when it came, he hung out of the window and was sick outside. Next morning he was seen hosing down the mess which was right down the whitewashed wall. He never mentioned drink again.

Being the author of these tales I have the privilege of saying nothing about myself!

A Hunger for the Hills

I used to give talks illustrated with slides (later moving on to PowerPoint) to various local groups on subjects such as the Scottish or other hill areas that I have wandered around. One talk on the Scottish hills illustrated bothies and camping as well as some of the hills where I had stories to tell. I called it Dossing and Stravaiging around Scotland.

Before relating an episode concerning that talk, I should point out that I am the world's worst cook. If a climbing hut has a smoke detector I am bound to give it a good test. My Club has even presented me at one of our annual dinners with a mounted model of a burnt sausage.

Anyway, I went to one local club to give the slide-show and waited while introductions were made. I was introduced as going to give a presentation entitled Dossing and Starving around Scotland. I thought about my cooking and decided that there was some truth in this.

Chapter 9 Ten Rounds of Munros & Beyond

Although I have been going out into the hills since the fifties, I was actually a late starter in knowingly climbing Munros. It is a trifle embarrassing to admit that I was born and brought up in Kirriemuir, only two miles from Sir Hugh Munro's home of Lindertis, but I was not aware of Munros until the late seventies. In 1978 Peter, a hill-climbing work colleague, enlightened me and we climbed many of the hills in Scotland together. Peter was born in East Anglia but has spent his entire working life in Scotland. He is very active in outdoor organisations and went on to become President of the Munro Society.

In autumn 1979, I met members of the recently formed Clyde Valley Mountaineering Club in the Beinn Damh bar in Torridon (it has been mentioned a few times that pubs seem to figure prominently in my stories) and the upshot was that I joined their Club.

At that stage, I had climbed about 150 Munros and one of the Club members, Bill, had climbed about half of that. He persuaded me to wait for him so that we could finish together. Another Club member, Donald, had completed climbing all the Munros some years previously except for Ben More on Mull. He did not want to be regarded as a Munro bagger so avoided that hill. Bill and I rather naughtily arranged to make our final Munro that hill and Donald could not resist the temptation to join us. We thus had a triple completion on June 6 1981 with over thirty relatives and friends, including my wife and two

Bill, Donald and I complete the Munros

daughters, and much bubbly. I do remember that one person present brought along a bottle of wine which shall remain nameless. I had never heard of it and have never seen it for sale anywhere. By the time that it had gone round everyone, the bottle was still about three quarters full. It was absolutely awful.

Some of us decided to extend the day by going down the east ridge and over A' Chioch and Beinn Fhada to our camp-site near Salen. A considerable quantity of alcohol had been consumed at the summit. When we climbed the east ridge a couple of years later we realised that it was quite exposed at places and we had been a trifle foolhardy two years before.

At this stage, I was well into my second round. I then started on the 2,500 footers, the Corbetts, completing them in 1984 on the same trip in which I finished my second round of Munros and first of subsidiary Tops. Incidentally, after the first round, I have always climbed the Tops in conjunction with the main summits as Munro's list was of the subsidiary Tops as well as the separate mountains. The completion hills and dates for my ten rounds of Munros and Tops are given in Appendix 1.

Completion of my third round in 1987 coincided with my thousandth Munro climbed. There was a bit of confusion at the start of this low key event with my wife, Eleanor, and two others. My mate Bill had misunderstood the starting point and was waiting a few hundred yards away. I told Eleanor and the fourth person to start up and I would find Bill and we would follow them. By the time that Bill and I started up the others had disappeared into the mist. We reached the summit and, after waiting for some time, decided that the others must have been and gone. We had just finished the celebratory wine when the other two arrived. They accepted the situation more calmly than I think I would have.

My fourth in 1989 was completed on the occasion of Bill's third round and Donald's second. Donald has since carried on to complete his hat-trick.

After that, rounds came on a fairly steady basis until I completed my eighth in 1996. At that point, I thought that it would be great to try to complete ten rounds in the same century as A.E. Robertson. I was asked if I would be willing to attempt it on behalf of a local charity and, in agreeing, decided to set a memorable date of 31 December 1999. The ninth completion came in mid-1998 so all was going well. I finished the last but one hill of the tenth round at the end of September 1999 in Knoydart and then had to ensure that I did not have a serious injury in the next three months.

I had chosen Schiehallion as my final hill. It is easily accessible and a straightforward walk except in really adverse conditions. I invited all the people who had climbed Munros with me and beavered away collecting money for the charity with a great deal of help from Club members and friends. I learnt a lot about the best times and places to voluntarily relieve people of their money.

The great day dawned cold and dry but the final approach on the roads was a trifle problematical because heavy snow had fallen overnight. However, over 60 people congregated at Braes of Foss and started up the hill. With the snow on the ground, a bitter wind and mist above 1,000ft., it was a chilly trip for me in the kilt. We met at the summit at 1pm to celebrate in the time-honoured way and included in the party were 19 Munroists which we reckoned might well have been a record. In addition, two other Munroists, one being Irvine Butterfield, had come part-way up the hill. My wife and one daughter were there with me and my other daughter had phoned from Australia that morning to wish me luck.

We then descended to the cars and retired to the Coshieville Hotel for more celebrations in a warmer environment. No evening entertainment had been arranged as I felt that people would want to get home for their own Hogmanay celebrations.

I was thrilled to raise nearly £5,500 for my charity and I only had two regrets. The first was that I was technically not completing ten rounds of Tops. Three new ones had been added in 1997 after I had climbed all the Tops for the tenth time. One of these has since been resurveyed as being less than 3,000ft.

Schiehallion – 31 December 1999

in height (Knight's Peak in the Cuillin). The other regret was that we could not carry on our celebrations into the evening. However, I had a germ of an idea for another celebration for the centenary of the first completion and we will come to that later.

There was a postscript to this occasion. A director of the charity, unbeknown to me, wrote to The Guinness Book of Records editor suggesting that the first to complete ten rounds might merit an entry in their publication. The first that I knew of it was when they sent me a letter with details of how to "prove" that one had climbed all the hills. The suggestions involved, firstly, written confirmation by unattached observers "close to or on the summit of each peak," of my ascents. Secondly, they required authentication of each and every climb and of my honesty by "two independent persons of some standing in the community," which rather ruled out climbing club members! Thirdly, a detailed log book must be kept and available for inspection (fair enough). They also required "a clearly labelled video showing part of each ascent." As many of my hills had been climbed when camcorders, especially small ones, were just a gleam in the eye this was clearly impossible. It was also a trifle late to suggest these 'rules' after I had completed the ascents. However, the most ludicrous suggestion was that, on each summit using a camera with a date stamp, two photographs were to be taken facing east from the cairn, two south, two west and two north as well as two of the cairn itself, all presumably regardless of weather conditions. I replied with constructive comments, the main one being that they should adhere to the Scottish Mountaineering Club list of compleaters (sic) which was based on trust. However, I went on to say that they were asking for ten photographs to be taken on each summit which, in my case was impractical after the event. However, if I had stuck to their 'rules', I would have had to send them 28,400 photographs (there were 284 Munros at that time). Their only concession was to reduce the required photographs to one or, if conditions allowed, two. That was many years ago and I have never heard from them again.

After I had completed the ten rounds, I was not far short of having topped 3,000 Munros. The Munro Society was planning in 2006 to celebrate the 150th anniversary of Munro's birth by having a climb of Driesh which was the nearest Munro to his estate near Kirriemuir. People would be signed in at the top. I managed to manipulate things so that this became my 3,000th Munro. Subsequent to that, a survey by the Munro Society resulted in Sgùrr nan Ceannaichean being reclassified as a Corbett and my total Munros climbed dropped back below 3,000. By pure chance I was out with the Munro Society doing a survey of Geal Charn up at Drumochter and, when updating my records, realised that I had, for the second time, hit 3,000 climbed – again with the Munro Society. Later still, a survey reclassified Beinn a' Chlaidheimh as a Corbett and my total again dipped below 3,000. I was on a meet with the Munro Society in Torridon when a climb of Beinn Alligin got me back to 3,000 yet again. I had thus reached 3,000 Munros climbed on three separate occasions, each time with the Munro Society and each time whilst wearing the kilt. As it is unlikely that any more Munros will be reclassified as Corbetts, I don't think that that is a record that can be equalled.

Chapter 10 A.E. Robertson Centenary

The ascent of all the Munros was first completed by Archibald Eneas Robertson on 28 September 1901 on Meall Dearg on the Aonach Eagach in Glen Coe. I had completed my ten rounds in the same century as him (31 December 1999) and felt qualified to organise a celebration on the centenary of AER's achievement. My idea was to centre it on his final hill.

During the midst of my preparations, I discovered that the Scottish Mountaineering Club was organising a centenary event. However, this was to be a dinner in Pitlochry which was well away from Glen Coe and in May which was well away from the centenary date. Theirs was a thoroughly enjoyable occasion but I felt that my own effort was still valid.

Robertson had not traversed the Aonach Eagach to climb his final hill but had ascended by a gully on the Glen Coe side. The gully had deteriorated over the years and it would be foolhardy to take a large party up it nowadays. Also, I was inviting anyone whom I had ever been on the hills with and the descent from Am Bodach might well have been beyond some. I reconnoitred the hill from the north and found a very practical approach from halfway between Glencoe village and Kinlochleven. This was in stalking territory but I explained the historical situation to the head-keeper and got clearance. I also arranged that vehicles could be parked in a caravan park close to the start-point. The actual centenary date was a Friday which would be inconvenient for many so I decided that one day late after 100 years was no great loss. Also, the celebration could not be allowed to splutter to an end after the climb – it must go on into the night.

I have spent a good few nights at Paddy Heron's bunkhouse and chalet complex at Onich and he was willing to set aside the chalets and several rooms in the bunkhouse for the weekend. It was a very fitting place to have a dinner because Paddy's father was Munroist number 21. At one time, it was thought that he might have been the first person to have a dog on the top of every Munro long before Hamish Brown did. However, this has now been discounted. My only claim is to have had the kilt up all Munros and Tops but I have no idea if this had already been done before. Paddy's son, David, set about organising printed menus and his daughter, fine cook that she is, came up with an excellent menu.

I had known Ian Mitchell of Mountain Days and Bothy Nights fame and Peter Drummond who wrote Scottish Hill Names since being on a trip with them to Morocco. They have each got many articles and books to their credit but what particularly attracted me was that they had collaborated to write a book on Robertson. They agreed to come and do a party piece.

I thus had my date, my hill, my route, my dinner, my entertainment and plenty of overnight accommodation. I only needed some people to accompany me. I sent out invites. I got some pretty poor excuses for not coming like "I'll be in Peru," "India," "Morocco," "Canada," and one, far more understandable, which said "It's too far from the south of England." I was delighted with the response. Sixty people attended of whom 49 committed themselves to going up the hill with 21 of those being Munroists.

We wakened up on the Saturday morning to a misty, wet day, which was not too promising, and drove round to the assembly point in Kinlochleven. We met up with those who had travelled up that morning. Some people went ahead to the starting-point whilst I waited for stragglers. I had sent out a description of the start-point relative to the caravan site. Unfortunately, there were two exits from the caravan park and the first party of four went out by the wrong gate and proceeded to go up the wrong glen. It was not until they reached the skyline at the west end of the Aonach Eagach that they realised that something was amiss. Meall Dearg was at the east end!

By the time that the rest of us started off, the rain had stopped and the mist was rising. A long string of people wended its way up the glen and ridge and

Some of the Munroists on Meall Dearg summit

eventually congregated on the summit – that is except for four people on a top two miles to the west wondering where the crowd was. When the first people arrived on the summit, there was still some mist but, as we celebrated, the mist drifted away and the sun came out. AER must have been looking after us. We had 21 Munroists on the top with a total group of 45.

I had dressed for the occasion in kilt, tweed jacket, shirt and tie and other people on the hills looked on in amazement at the crowd. My wife Eleanor and Julie my elder daughter had no trouble in getting to the top which really pleased me. Jenny, my younger daughter, had wakened up with such a sore throat that it was not sensible for her to go up.

There was a liquid celebration on the top and then we started down in dribs and drabs. Several parties continued along the Aonach Eagach and some went on to a nearby Corbett. Well down the hill, I met Peter, one of the four who had gone the wrong way, coming up. He had completed his Munros the day before on the actual anniversary. I turned round and accompanied him to the summit so he made the 22nd Munroist in our party to top out that day.

The dinner was a great success and seemed to be enjoyed by all. Ian and Peter's party-piece, a skit based on AER trying to enter heaven went down exceedingly well. It was subsequently well-received at the Kendal Film Festival but we could claim a world premiere! I added my bit with some stories backed up by appropriate slides. Nice things were said by Irvine Butterfield and others and several old friends were meeting for the first time in years. Celebrating and reminiscing went on well into the Sabbath but I don't think that AER would have minded.

Ian Mitchell as St. Peter

Chapter 11 Thoughts on Munro's Tables

When, in 1891, Sir Hugh Munro published his Tables of Scottish mountains exceeding 3,000ft. in height, maps were somewhat rudimentary and many if not most heights were only approximate. He included several anomalies whereby some subsidiary tops were shown as being higher than their associated mountains for reasons which have never been clearly explained. Additionally, various names and locations were incorrect. In this respect, it is interesting that over a century later, grid references, heights and names are still being changed. Sir Hugh recognised these shortcomings and his card system contained many subsequent corrections but he died before revised Tables were issued. It is thought that the 1921 edition largely if not totally reflected his planned changes. What does seem to be clear is that he was planning a tidying-up exercise having collected additional information over nearly 30 years since the original list had been published. As we know, he never defined in absolute terms what, in his view, determined a mountain and a subsidiary top. It is my personal opinion that this period of time had allowed him to review his list and come up with what he hoped were his final changes. He had better information available from maps and aneroid figures on heights and had had time to reflect on his subjective decisions as to what constituted mountains and tops. I think that, had he lived to issue an update, the next revision would have been his final list of three thousand-footers bar any future changes due to resurveying.

The Scottish Mountaineering Club's justification for continuing changes to the Tables is that Munro himself planned to make changes but I disagree with this (continuing) concept. They have every right to do what they want with the Tables because they commissioned them in the first place. I submit that the only valid changes to the 1921 Tables should be based on re-survey. As an example, Sir Hugh knew what Beinn Eighe or Buachaille Etive Mòr looked like but decided to call them individual mountains. They, along with several others, have each since been deemed to be two mountains.

Three mountains and one top re-measured as being over 3,000ft. had been introduced to the 1921 list and six tops removed as being under 3,000. Of the six, two have since been reintroduced after subsequent resurveying. Additionally, five summits had been relocated to nearby higher locations. This indicates to me that Munro was only changing his list on the basis of resurveying.

From 1921 up to the 1974 Tables all entries to and removal from the

Mountains and Tops were due to resurveying with one exception. This was the lower of two east tops of Sgùrr nan Ceathreamhnan. This was deleted for some inexplicable reason in 1974 although it is over 3,000ft. Otherwise, other than changes due to resurveys, the 1974 list was identical to the 1921 one (so far as I can see) although there were many changes to coordinates and names.

Thus, from 1921 to 1974, only 16 changes to the list of Mountains and Tops were made, all but one for re-survey reasons, and two of these have subsequently been reversed. In contrast, since 1974, there have been about 120 changes and of these only about a dozen were based on re-survey. The 1981 edition made wholesale changes which, in my view, altered the Tables so significantly that, from then on, they should be referred to as 'based on Munro's Tables.' However, the official changes of 1981, 1984, 1990, 1997 and 2021 are now so set in stone that my proposition would presumably be unacceptable.

Whilst the reversion to the original concept is probably a lost cause, I include as Appendix 2 a list of all hills which have been in the Tables at some time or other but are no longer included. I have heard many people refer to these as demoted hills but I think that this is somewhat derogatory. A better description is to refer to them as reclassified. Climbing those will ensure that you have covered everything in Munro's list. You might be surprised to find that it contains 95 entries although some of these appeared after the 1921 Tables and were therefore not acknowledged by Munro.

Finally, to end on a controversial note, I have always contended that Munro produced a list of mountains and subsidiary tops. Very shortly after the first Tables were produced in 1891, people started to refer to the separate mountains as Munros. However, I maintain that he produced a list of hills, some being mountains and others tops. In my opinion, to call oneself a Munroist one should have completed the full list – whether that is solely the current list or should include Munro's reclassified hills is for the individual to decide.

Epilogue

Many years ago I devised a computer system to store my climbing details. For those who perhaps are interested in such facts, I have summarised the information in Appendix 3. I make no apology for including my achievements because most people I chat to want to know this sort of thing.

Round about 1995, having completed the Corbetts and Donalds ten years before, I became aware of the Grahams, the Scottish hills between two and two and a half thousand feet and I completed them early this century. One of the delights of Grahams is that, in many places, you could climb one in the morning, have a pub lunch and climb another in the afternoon. On a strenuous summer day, you could climb a third between dinner and pub.

Quite recently, Alan Dawson who produced the list of Grahams, changed the minimum height for qualification from 2,000ft to 600m. This increased the Grahams from 219 to 231. I had climbed these 12 extra as Marilyns so I could still call myself a Grahamist. I do sympathise with those who had climbed the original 219 hills on the list and then found that they had not climbed all of the new list.

Round about the turn of the century, I became aware of Alan Dawson's list of Marilyns – all hills in Scotland, England and Wales with a minimum ascent of 150m on all sides, regardless of height. Part of the incentive to tackle this list was that, having climbed most hills over 2,000ft., I already had a good start on it. Many people have commented that they must be very boring but the lower ones get you into new territory and many are marvellous viewpoints, especially those close to the sea. They have the added attraction that these lower ones are invariably clear which is more than can be said for the bigger hills. I was on my ninth round of Munros and Tops before I could claim to have had a view from the top of each one. I've climbed all but about four of the 1,550 or so Marilyns but the last three on St. Kilda are beyond my aging bones and I doubt if I will get up to the wilds of Cape Wrath to climb one more recently discovered. I say 'about four' not climbed because several in England have been moved to nearby higher locations since I climbed them. It's a long way to go to climb a hill that has been 'moved' across a couple of fields.

In this same period early this century, as I completed the Grahams, I also climbed the Wainwrights and outliers and the English and Welsh 2,000-footers as well as many of the higher hills in Ireland. Appendix 1 summarises the hill lists that I have completed and when.

Quite a group of people were nearing the completion of climbing the Marilyns and Mark Jackson extended Dawson's list by reducing the minimum drop on all sides to 100m. As they had a prominence of at least 100m he called them Humps (Hundred & Upwards Metres Prominence). This list almost doubled Dawson's one to nearly 3,000 hills. I have climbed over 80% of them but the remainder are scattered around at a considerable distance from home. Other commitments make it harder and harder to get enough time to embark on a longer trip to faraway hills.

A further list of hills with thirty metres drop has been produced. They are called Tumps (Thirty & Upwards Metres Prominence). This list contains over 17,000 hills. As well as maintaining my own more detailed log of hills climbed, I now maintain a record on the hill-bagging.co.uk website. This site uses the information on the Data-base of British and Irish Hills to provide users with their progress on nearly 50 hill lists. The system credits me with over 3,200 of the Tumps but these are mainly hills that I have climbed as Munros and other hills over 2,000-feet plus lower Marilyns.

I must have been over many other Tumps during my years walking the hills. However, my logs are unlikely to have mentioned them. At my age, I am not going to scour my logs and maps to identify those that I may have climbed.

Incidentally, I have always thought that the name, Marilyns, for hills with a prominence of over 150m to be a bit facetious. In line with Humps and Tumps, I feel that a better term would have been Clumps, Cl being the Latin for 150. After all, clumps, humps, and tumps are all associated with the hills.

Mainly since I retired 25 years ago, I have been to several places in the world which attracted me. Going abroad now is increasingly unlikely because of the cost of insurance once you reach eighty. However, I never tire of the Scottish hills. The smaller ones are featuring more now but the bigger hills still get attention. As long as my health holds out, I'll keep going back to the hills. In an unguarded moment, I was heard to comment that Torridon would be a nice place for my ashes so my final trip could be amongst the Am Fasarinen pinnacles.

I have been storing my recollections on a computer for many years and they cover a period of about sixty years. I have thought about writing a book for many years but kept putting it off whilst still active in the hills. My body tells me that my really long continuous climbing days are behind me. I find that over such a day my legs get unsteady. However, climbing several smaller hills over the same number of hours with car or bike between them is no problem.

I have really enjoyed putting this book together and I hope that you enjoyed reading it.

Appendix 1 My Hill Lists Completions

Hill List	Last Hill	Date
Munros Round 1	Ben More, Mull	06.06.1981
Furths Round 1	Brandon Mountain	28.09.1981
3 Peaks Round 1	Ben Nevis	04.07.1982
Munros Round 2	Carn na Chlamain	04.08.1984
Tops Round 1	Carn na Chlamain N.Top	04.08.1984
Corbetts	Beinn Mheadhonach	04.08.1984
Tops Round 2	Beinn na Socaich	17.11.1984
Furths Round 2	Brandon Mountain	30.05.1985
Furths Round 3	Brandon Mountain	04.08.1987
Munros & Tops Round 3	Ben Vorlich(Arrochar)	15.08.1987
Donalds	Innerdownie	02.09.1987
Munros & Tops Round 4	Beinn Bhuidhe	13.08.1989
Munros & Tops Round 5	Beinn Bhuidhe	02.06.1990
Munros & Tops Round 6	The Devil's Point	06.06.1992
Munros & Tops Round 7	Sgùrr nan Eag	27.05.1994
Munros & Tops Round 8	Bla Bheinn	26.05.1996
Munros & Tops Round 9	Beinn na Lap	02.05.1998
New Donalds	Uamh Bheag	08.01.1999
Munros & Tops Round 10	Schiehallion	31.12.1999
Grahams	Beinn Gaire	06.06.2009
Wainwrights	Haystacks	14.11.2009
Ochils 300m hills	The Nebit	18.04.2010
British Isles P600s	Slieve Snaght	22.06.2010
Wainwright Outliers	Hare Shaw	06.03.2011
English 2,000 foot hills	Gragareth	15.05.2011
Welsh 2,000 foot hills	Pen-y-Helgi Du	05.10.2011
3 Peaks Round 2	Ben Nevis	07.06.2013

1. Carn na Chlamain N.Top is no longer in the Tables
2. I have climbed 99.7% of the Marilyns (the list is still changing).
3. I have climbed about 82% of the Humps.
4. I have recorded climbing about 19% of the Tumps.
5. Especially large hills that I have climbed are Kilimanjaro, Toubkal, Mount Whitney and Humphrey's Peak.
6. Beinn Gaire was my last British Mainland Marilyn as well as my last Graham.

Appendix 2 Hills Out of Munro's Tables

95 summits have at some time featured in the Tables but are not in the 2021 edition. Asterisked summits are known to have been surveyed and are under 3,000 feet. Others may have been surveyed but are mainly hills deemed to be unworthy of inclusion by the Scottish Mountaineering Club. Of these 95 hills, after survey, nine were found to be at a higher nearby location. Names, grid references and heights have changed slightly over the years.

No.	Sect	Hill Name	Grid. Ref	Ht (m)
1	1	Beinn an Lochain*	NN218079	901
2		Ben Lui NW Top	NN265264	1127
3		Cruach Ardrain SW Top	NN407211	1031
4		Stob Garbh SE Top	NN413217	925
5		Creag a' Bhragit	NN447224	914
6		Beinn a' Chroin W Top	NN385185	938
7	2	Meall Garbh (old location)	NN651515	c965
8		Meall Luaidhe	NN656510	925
9		Meall Buidhe SE Top	NN501489	916
10		Sron dha-Murchdi	NN611404	927
11		Beinn nan Eachan E Top	NN574383	948
12		Creag na Caillich*	NN563377	914
13		Stob an Fhir Bhoga	NN411372	1030
14		Top of Coire Dubh	NN378449	959
15	3	Ben Starav SE Top	NN128425	1068
16		Sron nan Giubhas	NN231462	974
17		Aonach Eagach (Stob Ghabhar)	NN236454	991
18		Màm Coire Easain	NN239499	1069
19	4	Carn Beag Dearg	NN171737	1006
20		Ben Nevis NW Top (old location)	NN159722	1211
21		Stob Coire an Fhir Dhuibh	NN208735	983
22		Stob Choire Claurigh N Top	NN262744	1134
23		Sron Garbh	NN508809	1023
24		Meall Garbh (old location)	NN371731	976
25	5	Meall a' Chaoruinn	NN646777	916
26		Sgairneach Mhòr (old location)	NN595728	963
27		Bruach nan Iomairean	NN601759	c972

No	Sect	Hill Name	Grid Ref	Ht (m)
28	6	Druim Sgarsoch	NN946835	954
29		Beinn Gharbh	NN853791	932
30		Carn a' Chlamain N Top	NN914761	952
31		Carn a' Bhutha*	NO034820	905
32		Carn nan Sac	NO119770	920
33	7	Creag Leachdach	NO211817	960
34		Lochnagar-Cac Carn Mòr	NO245857	1150
35		Craig of Gowal (old location)	NO227817	983
36	8	Diollaid Coire Eindart	NN905928	974
37		Druim nan Bo	NN873921	918
38		Stob Coire nan Lochain	NN940997	1230
39		Leachd Riach or Leth-creag	NN922939	991
40		Ben Macdui N Top	NN991995	1295
41		Stob Coire Sputan Dearg	NN998985	1249
42		Fiacaill na Leth-choin	NH975034	1083
43		Creag an Leth-choin N Top	NH969039	1026
44		Fiacaill Coire an t-Sneachda	NH988032	1125
45		Fiacaill a' Choire Chais	NH999039	1141
46		Sron a' Cha-no	NJ016066	1028
47		Beinn Mheadhoin SW Top	NJ018011	1163
48		Little Cairngorm	NO020973	1040
49		Big Brae	NJ159033	939
50		Stob Bac an Fhurain	NJ137034	1076
51		Mullach Lochan nan Gobhar	NJ143022	1105
52		Stuc Gharbh Mhòr	NJ147013	1120
53		Stuc Gharbh Mhòr (old loc'n)	NJ146017	1112
54		Stob Dubh an Eas Bhig	NJ133002	1063
55		Ben Avon SW Top	NJ125013	1135
56		Beinn a' Bhuird S Top (old loc'n)	NO090978	1177
57		A' Choich	NO096987	1050
58	9	Creag Meagaidh E Top	NN424875	1115
59		Creag Mhòr	NN444873	1069
60		Stob Poite Coire Ardair E Top	NN437892	1051
61		A' Bhuidheanach	NN481907	967

No	Sect	Hill Name	Grid Ref	Ht (m)
62		Sneachdach Slinnean	NH621027	919
63		Carn Ballach NE Top	NH647048	918
64	10	Am Bathaich*	NG988075	c900
65		The Saddle (Trig Point)	NG934131	1010
66		The Saddle (W Top)	NG928128	968
67		The Saddle (E Top)	NG938130	958
68		Sgùrr na Creige*	NG936137	c900
69		Faochag*	NG954123	c900
70	11	Mullach Fraoch-choire NE Top	NH100175	1047
71		Carn a' Mhadaidh-Ruaidh	NH141148	922
72		Sgùrr nan Ceathreamhnan E Top	NH065225	960
73		Stob Coire nan Dearcag	NH071225	940
74		Creag nan Clachan Geala	NH043232	998
75		Mullach na Dheiragain E Top	NH087266	932
76		Stob Coire Coulavie	NH111240	1069
77		Ciste Dhubh	NH114246	1109
78		Stob Coire na Cloiche	NH075227	915
79	12	Rudha na Spreidha	NH163356	1057
80		Creag a' Chaoruinn	NH168338	972
81		Braigh a' Choire Bhig N Top	NH158337	1013
82		An Riabhachan NE Top	NH139348	1117
83		Creag Toll a' Choin	NH131453	1006
84		Sgùrr nan Ceannaichean*	NH087480	913
85	13	Creag Dhubh	NG986607	c914
86		Choinneach Mhòr (old loc'n)	NG950601	954
87	14	Slioch (Trig Point)	NH005688	980
88		Corrag Bhuidhe Buttress	NH066831	945
89		Beinn a' Chlaidheimh*	NH061775	914
90	15	An t-Socach - Ben Wyvis	NH471681	1004
91		Glas Leathad Beag W Top	NH485705	923
92		Fiaclach - Ben Wyvis	NH496711	920
93		Ceann Garbh (old location)	NH266831	937
94	17	Sgùrr Dearg (Cairn)	NG443216	978
95		Knight's Peak*	NG471254	914

Appendix 3 Hill & Weather Statistics

(as at end 2022)

Hill climbed most times (Cairngorm)		17
Most ascents of a Munro before a summit view (Moruisg)		8
Most ascents of a Top before a summit view (Sgoran Dubh Mòr)		9
Most outings in a year (1983)		89
Most hills in year (1989)	189 Munros, 157 Tops, 2 Corbetts	348
Total days over 2,000 feet		1,729

Total hills over 2,000 feet climbed:	Munros	3,029
	Tops	2,344
	Corbetts	312
	Grahams	259
	Donalds*	198
	Furths	151
	Total ** (2,521 solo)	**6,293**

* Excludes Donalds which are also Corbetts or Grahams
** Excludes 547 climbs of hills removed from the Tables

Most popular month for hills climbed (May)	863
Least (December)	259

The weather breakdown for the 6,293 hills is as follows:

Perfect weather with little or no breeze	1,246	
As above but windy	333	
Overcast & dry with little or no breeze	854	
As above but windy	1,002	
Changeable with little or no breeze	384	
As above but windy	567	
Wet or misty with little or no breeze	506	
As above but windy	865	
Very wet and misty with little or no breeze	197	
As above but windy	339	6,293

The numbers in the last two weather categories are probably artificially low because if it was that bad before starting, I probably retired to the pub!

These figures do not include hills below 2,000ft. or any Marilyns or Humps which are above 2,000ft. but not in the above categories.

Acknowledgements

To Clyde Valley Mountaineering Club members without whom many of the events in this book would never have happened.

To Derek Sime for his proof-reading, improvement of my old photographs and providing much information about how to create this book and get it into print.

To Hamish Brown for his Foreword, proof-reading and advice.

To Jeremy Fenton for assembling the text and photographs into a publishable document.

To Alex Thomson for advice on creating a self-published book.

To Roderick Manson for assistance in creating Appendix 2 and proof-reading.

To the unrecorded photographers of the 8 images not taken by me.

To the many friends who have pressed me to create this book probably because they are fed up hearing the stories so many times.

Lastly, to my wife Eleanor, who put up with my many disappearances to the hills or to the computer to create *Wandering in the Hills in a Kilt.*